W9-BKU-562

The Cruelty
of Depression

The Cruelty
of Depression

On Melancholy

Jacques Hassoun, M.D.

Translated by David Jacobson
Foreword by Michael Vincent Miller, Ph.D.

ADDISON-WESLEY

Reading, Massachusetts

Many of the designations used by manufacturers and sellers to distinguish their products are claimed as trademarks. Where those designations appear in this book and Addison-Wesley was aware of a trademark claim, the designations have been printed in initial capital letters.

Library of Congress Cataloging-in-Publication Data

Hassoun, Jacques.
[Cruauté mélancolique. English]
The cruelty of depression : on melancholy / Jacques Hassoun ;
translated by David Jacobson ; foreword by Michael Vincent Miller.
    p.   cm.
Includes bibliographical references.
ISBN 0-201-59046-8
1. Depression, Mental.   2. Melancholy.   I. Title.
RC537.H3613   1997
616.85'27—dc21   97-20072
                                                                       CIP

Translation of *La Cruauté mélancolique*

English translation copyright © 1997 by Addison Wesley Longman, Inc.
Foreword copyright © 1997 by Michael Vincent Miller

Addison-Wesley is an imprint of Addison Wesley Longman, Inc.

Jacket design by Suzanne Heiser
Text design by Irving Perkins Associates
Set in 11-point Bembo by Pagesetters

123456789-DOH-0100999897
First printing, September 1997

Find us on the World Wide Web at
http://www.aw.com/gb/

Contents

THROUGHOUT THIS BOOK, both foreword and text, the pronouns "he" and "him" are used to refer to the melancholic subject. This usage intends no prejudice, but is simply a matter of stylistic expediency.

Foreword

by Michael Vincent Miller

HAS THE AGE OF ANXIETY, as W. H. Auden named the period following World War II, now been succeeded by the Age of Depression? Certainly there are ample signs in our culture, from best-selling memoirs by depressed authors (William Styron's 1990 book, *Darkness Visible,* is perhaps the most famous of a growing shelf of such books) to the booming business in antidepressant drugs (and, of course, best-sellers about these as well). Depression has overtaken anxiety as our presiding discontent. It is a mood swing that reflects a change in the weather of civilization. Whereas anxiety accompanied the development of modernism, signifying our restless anticipation of impending social catastrophe, depression seems to be the typical postmodern malaise, a chronic bad mood at the end of the Cold War. Even as the threat of nuclear holocaust subsides, it's as though we have already been through too much.

This spiritual change can be illuminated by considering an essential difference between anxiety and depression. The anxious person is tilted toward the future in a state of agitated waiting for some nameless but dreaded coming event. Depressives fix their gaze on misfortunes that have already happened. They suffer from a kind of black nostalgia. Remaining disillusioned, after all, is a way to hold on to one's past losses. So are endless lamentation and self-recrimination. Wordsworth caught perfectly in a pair of lines the moment that sets the stage for depression: " 'Tis done, and in the after-vacancy/We wonder at ourselves like men betrayed." That single word *after-vacancy* speaks volumes about the inner life of depression. The seriously depressed person never stops living in an after-vacancy.

The psychotherapist must teach his or her patients to tolerate a measure of both—anxiety, so that they can live in time, which means facing uncertainty about what comes next; depression, at least temporarily, so that they can say good-bye to the therapist. Thinking about emotions like anxiety and depression in relation to time and history, to social life as well as individual life, however, seems much more connected to an older psychological tradition than it does to our own present attitude. Nowadays we tend to regard depression as a congenital disease caused by a biological endowment gone awry in certain individuals. According to this view, depression is a defect in how the brain functions, and the depressed suffer not from their past experiences, but from a statistical pattern of inheritance.

No doubt the new science of depression has hit upon important truths. Its recent practical fruits, known as the S.S.R.I.s (selective serotonin re-uptake inhibitors)—Prozac is the most well-known and commonly prescribed among them—have proven themselves able, if not altogether to cure depression, to counter it effectively, sometimes to an uncanny degree. The restoration of well-being now seems to require little more than swallowing so many micro-grams per day. Certainly no humane, pragmatic clinician can afford to ignore the relief antidepressants can bring. What is more troubling, though, is that at the level of culture the brilliant successes of psychopharmacology tempt us to take brain chemistry for the whole story. We end up with a narrow view of depression, which leaves out its mystery and metaphysical horror—the terrible waste but also the sometimes astounding creativity that can emerge from this dark cave in the human condition.

Every emotion, even the most unpleasant, contains the possibility of self-knowledge. Sadness informs us that the loss was important;

anger alerts us that the person in our path is an obstacle. Depression can be the most chastening state imaginable: it throws us back on our deepest sorrows and feelings of helplessness. What it may tell us about our limitations, our fears of abandonment, failure, and death, ought not to be narrowed too quickly to a matter of neurotransmitters flowing between synapses.

Jacques Hassoun, a distinguished French psychiatrist and psychoanalyst, wants us to reconsider that fading older tradition and its humanistic and ethical implications in a new light. *The Cruelty of Depression* (originally published in France as *La Cruauté mélancolique*) belongs to a venerable strain in Western thought, extending from Socrates to Freud, which considered a philosophical journey into one's own soul a prerequisite to self-improvement. In this sense Hassoun's book is a reminder, but it is also a highly original reformulation. As a man of medicine, he has had plenty of experience with the thorniest problems of treatment through working with profoundly disturbed mental patients in hospitals and clinics. But he is also a man of letters, the author of many books ranging from clinical investigation to political speculation, from psychoanalytic metatheory to cultural criticism. *The Cruelty of Depression* is the latest of twelve books he has published, although the first to appear in English.

In *The Cruelty of Depression,* Hassoun rejects the current overuse of the word *depression,* and turns to a much older name, *melancholy,* to describe the same distressing symptoms. One can see why. *Depression* has a slightly mechanical connotation—one depresses a lever to switch off a circuit. It also suggests something almost geologic in its inevitability, like a low place that is simply there, a concavity in the landscape of one's personality. Although melancholy may strike one as a quaint idea in a high-tech world, it connects us to a cultural past when such elusive yet durable misery commanded not only respect but even a touch of awe.

The sound of the word *melancholy* has a kind of poignant reach that suggests something beyond what *depression* conveys: *Melancholy* resonates with a sense of secret inner tragedy, of Byronic wounds. It hints at brooding from which one unmistakably suffers yet which also could be, one imagines, the wellspring of poetry or philosophy. One thinks of the pre-Socratic thinker Heraclitus, who was known as the melancholy philosopher, and of Shakespeare's Hamlet, the most melancholy of princes. Aristotle and Montaigne were prominent among those who felt that only melancholics could be philosophers. Kierkegaard, who managed to anticipate almost every modern feeling, gave melancholy an existential setting in his book *Repetition,* defining it as a state in which one lives in the present moment as though the worst future one can dream up has already happened (a notion, in fact, that turns out to be similar in ways to Hassoun's psychoanalytic interpretation). Freud, who invented our therapeutic outlook, joined this esteemed group when he wrote "Mourning and Melancholia," the first attempt to provide a theoretical foundation (as we understand theory. Robert Burton, in the seventeenth century, produced a sprawling work of scholarship, but not exactly a theory, called *The Anatomy of Melancholy*) for what we now diagnose as depression.

If the foregoing strikes one these days as bordering on a romantic treatment of mental anguish (the romantic sensibility itself may be a cover for being depressed), this does not mean that Hassoun (or Kierkegaard or Shakespeare) is unaware of the cost in pain that depression involves. In any event, the scientific attitude breeds its own romantic hopes; it's just that we have passed from a romanticization of certain illnesses—tuberculosis and neurasthenia were two late nineteenth-century fellow travelers alongside melancholia—to a romance of cure. Witness Peter Kramer's *Listening to Prozac,* for example. As I see it, the task that Hassoun sets himself is to face down our determinism and replace it with a contemporary vision of melancholy that would make perfect sense to Shakespeare or Kierkegaard: Hassoun's major thesis is that depression, or melancholy, is not simply an illness but a passion, or better yet, a passion so desperate and blocked that it is almost the inverse of a passion, a passion of absence. That Hassoun would develop such an emphasis is not altogether surprising, since one of the books that he published not long before this one was *Les Passions intraitables,* a study of how passion can turn up in multiple guises to take possession of one's being. To claim that depression is closely, if negatively, related to passion leads one down a quite different path than the one newly cleared by biological research. Consider, for example, the following statements by two thoughtful nonclinical authors. Before his death, the literary critic Anatole Broyard remarked that "The modern serious novel is an attempt of the writer to identify his depression." And an influential Italian sociologist, Francesco Alberoni, wrote that "Like every other movement, falling in love springs, at the individual level, from an excess of depression."[1] If these comments sound a little strange to our ears, neither of them would mystify Hassoun. Both depend on the notion that depression, like passion, involves the creation of meaning.

Does it indeed make sense to speak of depression as meaningful, since meaning is not given but made? Donald W. Winnicott, one of the best among the leading psychoanalytic thinkers, certainly thought so; he wrote that "Not everyone admits that there is a psychology of depression at all. For many people (including some psychiatrists) it is almost a religious belief that depression is bio-chemical, or a modern equivalent of the black bile theory. . . . But for me there is a meaning to mood."[2] Winnicott did not say much about what he thought this meaning might be. Hassoun's entire book, however, is a serious attempt to build a theory around that question.

Passions are not just blind instincts; they are experienced as inherently meaningful. However much they may sweep us beyond any hope of feeling in control, they are more than randomly assigned facts of our nature. To be passionate about anything calls

---

[1] Francesco Alberoni, *Falling in Love,* trans. by Lawrence Venuti (New York: Random House, 1983), 152.

[2] D. W. Winnicott, "The Value of Depression," in *Home Is Where We Start From: Essays by a Psychoanalyst,* ed. by Clare Winnicott, Ray Shepherd, and Madeline Davis (New York: W. W. Norton & Company, 1986), 74.

upon will and imagination. One could interpret both Broyard's and Alberoni's propositions as telling us that love and art may be among our deepest struggles to master the problem of depression. How? By giving us a reason to live. By transforming a shadowy dreadful passion that robs one of a world into productive passions that connect one to the world. This possibility implies clearly that depression, no matter what its roots in the molecules, is a facet of the human condition that can be drawn upon for the creation of culture, an act that requires a good deal more from us than our neurobiology.

Freud had no doubts that depression was meaningful and thus could be understood. His conception, most fully spelled out in his seminal essay "Mourning and Melancholia" goes roughly like this: Melancholy, or depression, occurs when conflicting impulses reach a standoff in an individual whose still developing or otherwise weakened personality cannot tolerate the loss of a loved one—especially a loved one upon whom he or she depends, such as a parent. First of all, there is the grief that comes with every significant loss. In certain cases, the loss may feel so unbearable that the person tries to resurrect the needed individual psychologically through a mental process that Freud called *introjection*. This process entails internalizing an image; it's essentially an attempt at identification with the character of the person who has vanished. The outcome is that the soul of the other, like a parasitic ghost, lives on in the hidden fantasy life of the one left behind.

In addition to grief, however, people who suffer a loss become enraged as though they had been deliberately abandoned, even if they know perfectly well that the loss occurred through sickness or accidental death. The unconscious, in Freud's view, is hardly judicious or rational in parceling out accusations. Since the original person who fired up the rage is no longer there to receive (and thus absorb) it, one turns it upon the internalized image, which means against oneself. In Freud's formulation, depression, or melancholy, is like a dormant volcano. Deep in its bowel, sadness and anger quarrel with each other, each blocking the other from getting the upper hand, so that they continue to smolder under the surface of the sufferer's personality. Only remnants of the battle reach consciousness. Generally these are knowable only as an overall feeling of unresolvable misery.

Hassoun draws heavily on these Freudian ideas, but he widens their scope to give them, if somewhat less precise applicability, a more poetic, metaphorical reach. As did Freud, Hassoun links depression to loss, but his concern is not focused specifically on the loss of a person. Instead he delineates a particular situation of loss resulting from circumstances that can occur near the beginning of a child's development. For Hassoun, depression—or melancholy, as he continues to call it—is the shadow thrown across consciousness by the loss of paradise. The paradisal landscape he has in mind is one every child must lose—the mother's nurturing breast. Melancholy is the consequence when neither the mother nor the child is able to tolerate or mourn the loss.

Of course, many psychological theorists of human development since Freud have recycled the opening lines of Genesis, casting Eden as life in the womb or at the breast. And nearly every psychoanalytic thinker has regarded weaning as an especially dramatic—or traumatic—event during a child's early period of growth. For Freud, weaning was a landmark in one's psychological as well as biological growth into individuality. But the child's actual experience of being weaned, Freud thought, was tinged with deprivation and dread. From the psychoanalytic perspective, anxiety and autonomy were born in the same moment, a volatile combination that would haunt all of an individual's future relationships. A later Freudian, Melanie Klein, the ancestor of what is now called psychoanalytic object relations theory, enlarged on Freud's emphasis to give the breast and weaning an even grander, more symbolic place in human psychological development. She spawned concepts that became highly influential in England and America: the "good" and "bad" breast, the child's paranoid and depressive reactions to it, and the importance of the child's introjected images of it in the unfolding of all relations of self to others.

Hassoun carries these forerunners' ideas further into a metaphorical thicket of complexities. Drawing on a line of thinking unique to French psychoanalysis, he not only uses the breast as a symbolic idea in his theory but insists that in the course of separating from the mother, the child also has to recontruct her breast into a symbol of profound psychological import, something that Hassoun calls the *lost object*. The importance of this lost object is not to be underestimated: without it, a child cannot survive the fall from Eden into a state of separateness, a state that Hassoun thinks of as becoming a *subject*.

Notions like the lost object and the subject, conceived in a highly specialized way in Hassoun's writings, require elucidation, especially for an English-speaking audience. Reading Hassoun is not easy. His writings have an affinity with those modern poets and philosophers, especially Continental ones, who can make for extremely difficult going at times. In part this comes from his own highly complex ideas; in part it is a function of a specialized language peculiar to French psychoanalysis.

The French do not imbibe their Freud straight, but take him as directed by the "French Freud," the astringent, obscure, intimidating figure of Jacques Lacan. Lacan's far-reaching Talmudic commentaries on Freud's writings—delivered in lectures, seminars, and essays—reshaped psychoanalysis into a radically new form of discourse. Where Freud was influenced by the idea of nature, which meant the Newtonian causal science and the biology of his time, Lacan almost completely alters this context. Lacan's so-called "return to Freud" filters the whole of psychoanalysis through entirely human-made structures, such as the transformational grids of linguistics and modern anthropology. The outcome is then elaborated with epistemological musings, metaphysical considerations, and close attention to textual performances in literature. The hold that Lacan's renovations have exercised not only on psychotherapy in France, but on the whole of French culture during the past few decades, is remarkable in its magnitude.

Besides what he took from Freud's writings, Lacan borrowed and revised several motifs that had captured the attention of psychoanalytic theorists just after Freud: an interest in how children's first preverbal fantasies help form their sense of reality; the concept of libidinal object relations, which delineates how adult attachments between people reflect the intensity of their earliest attachments; and the growing concern with countertransference, i.e., the role that the life experience and character of the analyst plays in therapy. These were among the topics that led Lacan to shift theory and treatment away from the isolated individual to the frontier of what goes on—or, more accurately, seems to go on—between people.

Beyond such matters, however, the position Lacan arrived at barely overlaps with contemporary psychoanalytic theory, because the latter concentrates on the issue of individual ego strength. Lacan was particularly critical of American ego psychology. His major concern was with the psychological formation of something he called the "subject," a concept that has its roots in Descartes and the subsequent critique of Descartes by the phenomenological philosophy of Husserl, Heidegger, and Sartre. Descartes had defined the existence of the subject through his famous *cogito,* "I think therefore I am." This was, Descartes had concluded, the bedrock of subjective experience, but it also created an unbridgeable split between mind and body, subject and object. The phenomenological critique attempted to reunify subject and object by placing both mind and body, self and nature, under the sway of subjective experience. Lacan's idea of the subject comes close to the phenomenologist's concept in many respects. But there is also a crucial difference: both Descartes and the later phenomenologists conceive subjective experience in terms of deliberate, conscious activity. Lacan is too much of a Freudian to settle there; for him, one's existence as a subject is essentially a formation of unconscious life.

Besides redefining subjectivity, importing it from its metaphysical status in philosophy, and transforming it to fit his vision of psychoanalysis, Lacan went after the concept of the object as well. Like subjectivity, the object had a place in philosophy—in debates, for example, between naturalistic and idealistic philosophers about the object of perception. But it had also become a key term in contemporary psychoanalysis: *Object* was the name psychoanalysis used for an entity or fragment from the world, capable of being internalized, which served as the aim of an instinct or drive. As was his wont, Lacan amalgamated motifs from philosophical and psychoanalytic traditions and integrated them into his own peculiar vision. Lacan's object has an almost unspecifiable status. It is not exactly in the world nor inside the self. It cannot be understood as belonging either to objective nature or to subjective fantasy. In effect it exists between the two, taking its place in a complex overall structure of one's relation to the otherness of the world.

This Lacanian object is inextricably linked to human desire. It is called into being by one's desire. At the same time, it is the object of such desire. Lacan's theories make up a psychology of relationship, not just of self, but the nature of connection between self and other, as he develops it, is at best ambiguous. Our basic condition, he emphasizes, is desire, which creates our experience of the world, but desire is never completely fulfilled. We can always strive to come closer, but, like the asymptotes of a parabola, we can never quite get there. At the risk of caricature, one could almost say that in Lacan's human landscape two people never quite make love—rather, two phantasms make love in a delirium of belief that they are contacting otherness.

A central aspect of Lacan's contribution was to bring into the foreground that which had not been much emphasized previously in psychoanalytic theory: language itself, the medium through which humans chiefly learn, communicate, form and sustain relationships with each other. In Lacan's view, bringing linguistic knowledge to bear on psychoanalytic theory and practice could provide analysts with a precise tool of exploration in fundamental areas where they had been operating with little beyond shaky intuition. If this sounds like an American emphasis on the quantitative, however, one must bear in mind that for Lacan language is libidinal, impassioned. It is full of fury and yearning. Language virtually *is* desire—our burning desire to meet, to address, to unite with the otherness of the world, which we can never fully attain. But this desire is life itself, at least it is the core, from Lacan's standpoint, of human psychological life.

Thus one comes to Lacan's most well-known radical elaboration of a Freudian idea—his intriguing proposition that "the unconscious is structured like a language." This assumption goes far beyond Freud's claim that dreams and other unconscious phenomena can be understood by interpreting them as a relationship between manifest (accessible to consciousness) and latent (unconscious) content. Lacan redefines the unconscious mind: it is no longer a repository of biologically driven instincts and repressed thoughts but a cultural construct, like grammar.

Such an idea probably could have come only from a Frenchman. On the one hand, the French language—in both sound and sense, with its silky elisions, its gift for nuance, its mellifluous flow of impressionistic images—seems somehow closer than other languages to the material one associates with the unconscious. This is why French literature slides so smoothly into the world of dreams, into a logic of associations, into alternate realities, even into vacancy, absence, nothingness. One feels this in poetry from Rimbaud to Mallarmé, in surrealism and dada, in the theater of the absurd, in the writings of Michaux and Artaud.

On the other hand, there is a counterpart to French dreaminess. No other culture loves subtle formal structure, whether in social life or art, more than the French. Take the plays of Racine or the poetry of Paul Valéry, who quit writing to study mathematics for ten years. For Lacan language was the bridge between the abstract structures of pure reason and the surreal logic of dreams. It seems fitting, then, that French psychoanalysis is a combination of wild speculation and strict schematic theories concerning the subterranean territories of unconscious life. This places it in a sharp, sometimes drastic, contrast to German, English, and American psychoanalysis, whose evolution has tended toward concentration on the well-defined, individual Ego.

So it has come about that in France, where psychoanalysis continues to flourish and to provoke vital intellectual debate, even as it fades from the American scene, theorists can still talk without embarrassment about so gross a portion of anatomy as the breast rather than limit themselves to chromosomes and neurotransmitters. They can ponder the contours of both body and soul rather than reduce states of mind to waxing and waning hormonal tides. They can still consider early human development and its intimate environment relevant to the production of disturbances like depression. It follows that there is still a place for a psychotherapy of self-knowledge grounded in a close collaborative relationship between therapist and patient, whereas American psychiatry increasingly emphasizes short courses of behavioral and cognitive engineering topped off with drug treatment—a program tailored to fit the requirements of managed care (one of the more sinister bureaucratic tropes of our era—sinister because it is seemingly innocuous. Language like this not only reflects but also contributes in small ways to our general decline of civility).

Lacan, in effect, invented a way of thinking about mental life and its vicissitudes that is at once Socratic and technical, speculative and precise. It focuses minute attention on the details of subjective experience in order to discover an orderliness in both the depths of interior life and the heat of interpersonal relationships. It thus has a strong social, as opposed to purely individual, dimension. Once upon a time such characteristics were dominant in American psychology as well. In the late nineteenth century, this view was a branch of philosophy, for instance in the work of William James. During a later period it was closely linked to sociology and anthropology, notably in the work of John Dewey and his colleagues at Columbia University and the University of Chicago. French psychoanalysis is closer to philosophical inquiry or literary criticism than it is to our insistent empiricism, our medical models of mental illness, and our current lack of clinical interest in the effect of social structures on individual psychological life.

Lacan's work and its influence on French intellectual life make up the theoretical background against which Jacques Hassoun writes. Although he borrows heavily from the intricate, sometimes frustratingly technical, sometimes poetic language of Lacanian analysis, he writes in his own quirky voice about concerns that are uniquely his own. There is great intensity in Lacan's writing, which conveys a sense of limitless penetration into the darkness, but it is cool, abstract, even icy at times. Hassoun is equally at home in the depths of the psyche, yet the temperature keeps rising in his books toward pleasure and sensuality when he captures life's more gratifying possibilities; toward the expression of an urgent, bemused sympathy when he contemplates his often deeply disturbed patients.

Psychoanalytic theory, in Hassoun's hands, resembles the metaphorical knowledge of poetry much more than it does scientific generalization from empirical data. His typical stylistic gesture is to stretch a metaphor, whether a Lacanian one or one of his own, to its breaking point, which gives a certain wild idiosyncracy to his writings on psychoanalysis. He discusses human development as though it were a situation of extremity, a series of apocalyptic arrivals at forks in the road on the way to forming a personality. His portrayals of various pathological mental states come across as ruined landscapes littered with pieces of bombed-out psychic architecture. When he writes about passion, he seems almost in the throes of it himself. Often his study of the melancholic temperament teeters precariously on the verge of excess. But it thus conveys the discrepancy one frequently senses between the relatively calm, if sad and withdrawn, social facade of the depressed person and the colliding, explosive forces about to boil over inside. Something similar is true of Freud, who found extraordinary Greek tragedies built around themes of incest, castration, and the murder of parents under the surface of decorous family relationships.

Although he is Parisian through and through—and moreover a Parisian who has carved out an important place for himself in French culture—Hassoun is not a native of France. An Egyptian Jew, he was born in Alexandria in 1936. He immigrated to France in 1954, settling first in Montpelier and then moving to Strasbourg a few years later. In the mid-sixties, he completed medical studies, which included a five-year internship in a psychiatric hospital where he treated psychotic patients. He went to Paris in 1965 and has remained there ever since. From 1967 to 1974 he worked as a psychoanalyst with the pediatric department of a hospital in a Paris suburb. During the watershed year of 1968, while France was caught up in the wave of student uprisings that affected political and cultural life all over the Western world, Hassoun was on the faculty of the University of Paris in Vincennes. He was torn between his empathy for the students' causes and his need to keep the teaching of psychoanalytic knowledge intact.

His psychoanalytic training took place at Lacan's famous institute, the École freudienne de Paris. He met and spoke often with Lacan, who had expressed interest in Hassoun's work, beginning with his observations as a pediatric psychiatrist, which resulted in a book titled *Entre la mort et la famille: l'espace-crèche* [Between Death and the Family: the Nursery], published in 1973. At present, Hassoun maintains an active private practice in Paris, teaches throughout Europe, and frequently visits the United States to lecture at universities and institutes, mainly on the two coasts. He is also cofounder and president of the influential French psychoanalytic group, the Cercle freudien. Meanwhile he turns out books on a wide range of subjects at an astonishingly rapid pace.

I first met Jacques Hassoun in 1992 when he visited an ongoing seminar at Harvard's Center for Literary and Cultural Studies to give a lecture on "Anxiety and Melancholy." Obviously the subject matter of *The Cruelty of Depression* was already on his mind. The seminar, concerned with the give-and-take between psychoanalysis and culture, was conducted by Barbara Freeman, a Harvard professor of English. What is significant about this is what it says about Lacan's influence in America. Thoroughly dominant in French clinical circles, Lacan has barely scratched the surface of psychotherapeutic theory and practice in America. On the other hand, Lacan's writings have become a staple in many humanities and social science departments in American universities, particularly where there is a strong feminist orientation. Why would feminist academicians be especially interested in Lacan's work? Probably because Lacan takes the position that gender is a social and psychic construct rather than a biological given, in contrast to Freud, who tended to define the feminine as a missing piece of male anatomy. Since then Hassoun has become an increasingly prominent spokesman for Lacanian analysis in the United States. In Boston alone, notorious for both its liberal politics and its conservative psychiatry, he has been a guest lecturer at departments of anthropology and political science, at psychoanalytic institutes, even at hospitals. Hassoun's warm-blooded version of Lacan's theory, fleshed out by his humanistic temperament and his fondness for explicating case histories (which are rare in the abstract theorizing of Lacan himself) has managed to generate more interest, at least in the U.S. metropolitan centers he now visits regularly, in the clinical possibilities of Lacanian psychoanalysis.

A haunting theme runs throughout Hassoun's work. Whether discussing psychology or politics, inner conflicts or social struggle, he is drawn toward images of exile. Perhaps there is a touch of his own melancholy in this—his flight from Egypt, his Judaism. The characters who seem to interest Hassoun the most, the ones who show up in case histories from his therapy files and the ones he borrows from films or novels to illustrate points of theory, range from psychotics to criminals to ordinary citizens, but they tend to have certain traits in common. They are given to nostalgia, a sense of cultural dislocation, a longing to feel at home. They remind one of the German sociologist Georg Simmel's definition of the stranger, "not . . . as the wanderer who comes today and goes tomorrow, but rather as the man who comes today and stays tomorrow." In Hassoun's social commentary, the question of exile is a way to probe the nature of citizenship and community. The theme of psychic alienation, however, permeates his psychoanalytic writings as well. His melancholics, for example, are despairing figures trapped at the dead-end of exile and fruitless quest to find their place in the world. "The melancholic never belonged to anyone, any place," he once told me. "He cannot separate from his exile and join the new world. This is his catastrophe."

Hassoun's preoccupation with exile plays an important role in his discussion about how depression originates in *The Cruelty of Depression*. If, as he indeed suggests, our coming to exist as separate individuals can be considered a kind of primal exile, a fall from an original home, it is an exile that every human has to survive. Psychologically, survival demands that we accept it and go about inventing a new way of being at home among the possibilities life offers—intimacy, work, friendship. In the case of melancholy, however, the fall into selfhood from union with the mother, Hassoun tells us, remains curiously incomplete. The clinically depressed individual's dilemma, the core of his misery, is that he does not accept it. He cannot. Accepting so momentous a loss requires one to suffer it all the way through, as one must suffer all losses, by grieving it fully. But the melancholic's ability to grieve has been profoundly disrupted, and this turns out to have tragic consequences: his love and work, his entire life for that matter, are consumed by a life-long search to get back into paradise, although that is not exactly how he experiences his situation. He knows only that his actual day-to-day existence is a living death, an unbearable emptiness in a parched wasteland. Hassoun portrays the melancholic's mental life as something resembling a lamentation in front of the closed gates to heaven, like those yearning tenors in Bach's cantatas.

In other words, the melancholic, for Hassoun, is trapped in a kind of paradox. He seems to do nothing but suffer; yet he does not know how to suffer. Grief, like the rest of our emotional palette, is a highly functional part of our animal nature. When one undergoes an important loss, it leaves a tear in the fabric that binds self to other. Whether one mourns in solitude, the way an animal slinks off to the woods to lick its wounds, or through public show at a wailing wall or dressed in sackcloth, the mourning does repair work on the injury to the self. In this respect, mourning is like recuperation after surgery. It is painful but necessary for healing, eventually enabling one to return to the world. The melancholic's tragic flaw is that he never learned to mourn. This will turn out to mean not only that he never returns to the world but, in Hassoun's view, that he never actually found it in the first place.

How does so shattering an event as losing one's world occur in the course of early human development? Hassoun's attempt to explain it takes him into dense Lacanian territory. And it will certainly be challenged as the most controversial part of his theory of depression.

Our first lessons in loss and mourning, according to Hassoun, are transmitted to the infant from the mother by her own experience of loss through the very act of giving her breast. Grief may be an innate emotion, but like other such expressive capacities, including language, it blossoms only through contact and exchange with a surrounding intimate environment. Otherwise it is liable to remain dammed up, a dormant potentiality that eventually atrophies, leaving only its trace—the residual, unending sadness that characterizes the feeling of depression. The crucial event in the drama that Hassoun makes of breastfeeding is that the mother actually surrenders her breast, which constitutes for her an emotional experience of giving and losing. What she loses is her breast as an emblem of her sexual identity, its symbolic magnetism as an aspect of her role in adult erotic intimacy. Her breast must now be converted into a new symbol, an object (in the Lacanian sense) that exists primarily between her and the child. To the extent that a mother, because of her anxiety or narcissism, cannot truly give the breast, but only goes through the motions, the child does not feel anything has been truly given to him, and there is nothing for him to lose. He is left unable to construct the next object in this chain, which Hassoun calls an *objet perte* [a lost object], whose existence is inextricably linked to his possibility of grieving. The purpose of this first experience of loss, in Hassoun's view, is to liberate the child's desire from the mother as sole object, so that he can now direct it toward the world.

This is an odd, convoluted formulation, yet Hassoun gives it a great deal of weight in his theory. Perhaps one can best grasp the distinction he wants to convey by recalling how maternal surrender is portrayed as a spiritual condition in innumerable medieval and

Renaissance paintings of the Virgin Mary nursing the infant Jesus. Giving the breast in such paintings is portrayed as a radiant act, almost a transport of concentrated love. The contrast would be with a preoccupied mother who offers her breast to the infant with mechanical indifference or resignation. The latter situation, for Hassoun, sows the seeds of future depression.

One of my favorite Italian jokes also captures some of the spirit of Hassoun's emphasis. It goes like this: God made Adam. Adam sat on a rock in Eden with his head in his hands. God appeared and asked, "Why do you look so sad, Adam? You have everything a man could want!" "I'm lonely," Adam replied. So God put Adam to sleep, extracted one of his ribs and made Eve. When Adam woke up, he found a beautiful naked woman standing in front of him, to which he responded by immediately sitting back down on the rock and again hanging his head in his hands. God reappeared in bewilderment and asked him, "Now what is it, Adam? Not only do you have everything here a man could want, but you told me that you were lonely, so I made you a beautiful wife." And Adam replied, "But first I need a mother!" The only thing that Hassoun might add is almost implicit in the joke—that Adam needs a mother in order to be able to lose her. Otherwise his depression most likely will become chronic.

Let me provide one more example. Not long after reading *The Cruelty of Depression* in its French edition, I went to see a retrospective exhibit of works by the great landscape painter Corot at the Grand Palais in Paris. The paintings were arranged, as is usually the case in exhibits of this type, in chronological order. One of the first paintings I saw, as I entered the first room, was a portrait of Corot's mother, a severe, thin-lipped, dry-looking woman, done in the 1830s. Scattered through the same room were a number of his early landscapes, also from the 1830s. They were heavy and dim in character, consisting mostly of classical landscapes, such as Roman scenes with statuesque buildings and figures. There was something dead about them; they contained no sensuality, almost no expression of feeling.

The next room held somewhat later paintings. These were more pastoral, depicting such themes as nymphs engaged in play or sprawling about in rural surroundings. In these paintings, the landscapes are still fairly dreary, but the nude female bodies glow with light. In one there is also a satyr whose head is thrown back to highlight the expression of glee on his face. This painting hung on a wall opposite some photographs of Corot himself, who looks somewhat like his mother, severe and depressed.

Further rooms contained Corot's later paintings. Some of these depicted scenes similar to earlier works—nude figures of women standing or lying about in the countryside; just as often in these works the women are dressed. The essential difference is that the luminosity now begins to spread beyond the bodies of the women to infuse the woods and meadows, the sky, the water. In other late paintings, new kinds of human figures and objects show up in the landscapes—farmers, laborers, boats, ploughs, people at work and at play.

One gets the feeling, in following the course of Corot's career, that he must have passed through stages of self-transformation which were reflected in his art—from a certain melancholy or depressed emotional deadness in his early classical work to an awakening of luminous desire and sensuality in the middle period, though it is still surrounded by an air of mournful darkness. If a certain intensity of concentration on the maternal female body is less evident in his late paintings, there is in its place a wider range of vitality and feeling for human society. I don't know if Corot's art itself was the agent of these transformations or whether his paintings mainly record other events in his life that brought about self-transformation. In either event, Corot's opus reflects a sense of the gradual release and then broadening of his desire to inhabit his world more fully.

Nevertheless, Hassoun's insistence on liberation from the maternal breast, accompanied by mourning the loss, may strike many people not only as a strange idea but also as an unpalatable one. For one thing, it is hardly politically correct, since it could be construed as a product of male fantasy. For another, it is vulnerable to being read as another instance of the kind of mother-bashing that has characterized much of our theorizing about human development. We have had almost every kind of bad mother in psychology: borderline mothers and schizophrenegenic mothers, intrusive mothers and passive-aggressive hostile mothers. Although these are arguable concerns, one can still extract the essence of what Hassoun attempts here—namely, to construct a metaphor for the first deep sense of belonging, of being at home, conveyed through a relationship in which love and sustenance are fused. Although this first landscape of belonging is inevitably lost, the capacity to belong in itself is not. In an interview that he gave to the French psychology magazine, *Le Journal des Psychologues*, Hassoun gave a sociological analogy for his theory of melancholy. He compared the generations of peasants in the Ardeche, who have managed to protect their land and their sense of belonging to it, to families who have undergone traumatic displacement due to war or deportation but have kept the pain of exile a secret from their children. The children grow up with an enigmatic sense of belonging nowhere.

Whatever one concludes about the mother-infant relationship as Hassoun describes it, there is unmistakable power in his tragic evocation of the melancholy personality. The journey to becoming a subject, in Lacan's meaning of that word, does not begin until paradise is lost. Hassoun once told a seminar at a hospital in Cambridge, Massachusetts, that mourning must precede one's consciousness of oneself as a subject. In the course of this transition, one finds a world that engages one's curiosity, wonder, hunger for experience, willingness to risk learning something new, ability to love. Moreover, it is easy to overlook the richness that Hassoun's Lacanian concept of the lost object introduces into his analysis of this transition. Isn't Proust's great novel filled with such lost objects, through which his own literary gifts come into full bloom in order to evoke the life of an entire society? The ultimate cruelty of depression for Hassoun is that the melancholic at the outset is prevented from crossing the barrier to those moments of self-realization in which creative desire is liberated as one enters the state of becoming a subject.

In a sense, the solution to living in a fallen world is to surrender one's will to the fact of unceasing change, to swim with, not against, the surf of growth and development. "Let the place of the solitaires/ Be a place of perpetual undulation," as the poet Wallace Stevens put it. Ernst Schactel, a developmental theorist, defined human psychological growth as "emergence from embeddedness," a fundamental movement that occurs at every important juncture from the womb or cradle to the lip of the grave. Conscious life is an emergence from—oblivion, perhaps? timeless bliss?—into history. But every step of growth involves a loss, since one leaves behind the comforting familiarity of what was. There are always growing pains. If one is willing to tolerate contingency, however, then the sense of adventure as one progresses from the known to the unknown territory outweighs the pain. Knowing that one can mourn a loss and then move on is a major psychological event that supports one's tolerance of uncertainty.

The problem for the melancholic is that he does not experience the progress but only the pain, because he has no place to go. When melancholics waken now and then to the life around them, they experience nameless fear, "an enigmatic internal danger," as Hassoun describes it in Chapter 5. Faced with uncertainty, they fill it in with the certitude that something terrible is about to happen to them. Then they subside back into their lifelessness. The anxiety was too much to bear.

Susan Sontag, who studied Walter Benjamin as a paradigmatic melancholic writer, spoke of how "something like the dread of being stopped prematurely" underlies his sentences. She is correct in her understanding of a basic depressive mechanism. In childhood the melancholic was in fact stopped prematurely and dreads its happening again forever after. As a consequence, the melancholic temperament does not reach out to the world—what's the use?— but curves back on itself (a condition that Martin Luther denounced as the primal sin: *en curvatus se,* to be curved in on oneself and therefore away from God). This is the negative of passion, if one takes passion to be absorption in some portion of one's world. To suffer the loss of loss means nothing less than to lose one's opportunity to have a world.

If Prozac works, do we really need Hassoun's book, with all its conjectures, its difficult ideas and metaphors, its closely knotted analysis? I say yes, we need it in the same way that we need poetry, fiction, moral philosophy, and cultural criticism. We will always need speculative, philosophical, and humanistic accounts of our lot—our dreams and ecstasies, our woes and defeats, our possibilities of transformation—presented in such books as *The Cruelty of Depression*. A dialectical war between knowledge as technique and knowledge as insight has long been waged on the cultural plains of Western civilization. It seems never-ending. The battle is particularly acute in the United States, where the elegant discoveries of science are often stripped, like cut flowers, of their roots in our beautiful humanistic traditions (which are then dubbed "soft-headed"). Then they are rapidly co-opted by bureaucratic centers of power and converted into the efficient technology demanded by competitive, profit-oriented economies.

Hassoun's book does not provide another means of self-help for the do-it-yourself recovery movement. He offers no guru-like advice at a time when many of us, too scared to listen hard to our own experience and reflect on it, seek solutions to the problems of life from surrogate parents. Nor does he offer an easy spiritual solution with which the New Age can further swell its trafficking in exotic religious traditions or marginal therapies. Much of our current psychology—and the same goes for our popular philosophy and theology—compounds the problem because it is readily digested and turned into techniques to counter the stresses of technology. This, at bottom, is just more of the same.

Since the nineteenth century at least, a voracious optimism, certain that the good life is just around the corner, has been an occupational hazard of the American way. Freud, for one, became worried when the United States digested psychoanalysis so promptly, while his own culture still continued to resist it. He was sure that Americans would vulgarize his discoveries. *The Cruelty of Depression* is probably exempt from that fate. It is too unusual, too meditative, too labyrinthine, perhaps even too personal a book. But so are the novels of Proust or Henry James. Such books add little to our repertoire of techniques; instead, they add something worthwhile to our sense of life itself.

Michael Vincent Miller
Cambridge, Massachusetts
June 1997

Acknowledgments

THE MELANCHOLIC RESISTS NAMING and turns any debt into an endless dirge over a massive guilt that lament only continues to feed. So let me lose no time in recalling my debts for the present work, which follows the basic outline of the seminar I gave at the Cercle freudien from 1990 to 1993. I wish to thank all those who, by their active presence there, allowed me to pursue my topic, especially those who, like Pedro Bendetowicz, Fabienne Biegelman, Karen Burtin, Michèle Dolin, Josée Jiederman, Monique Novodorsqui, Daniel Koren, Miren Arambourou, Chantal Maillet, and Nicole Tuffelli, strengthened various hypotheses of mine through their participation.

I would also like to thank the journal *Esprit* and my colleagues at *Apertura* for having accepted and published parts of what would eventually form certain chapters of this book,[1] as well as the groups of psychoanalysts at Metz, Besançon, Grenoble, Lyon, Montréal, Boston, and New York who helped me continue along some of the paths my thought was taking.

Finally, I should mention Anne Longuet-Marx and Edith Wolf, who in drawing my attention to Herman Melville's "Bartleby" and Robert Walser's *Institute Benjamenta*, respectively, allowed me to frame and thus conclude these investigations.

---

[1] Chapter 1, Janus the Melancholic; Chapter 2, "From one passion to the other," and Chapter 5, Where Passion and Anxiety Meet: The Wait.

The Cruelty
of Depression

"*Do you not know, Madame,*" [Sti Horg] *said slowly, visibly embarrassed and unsure whether to continue speaking or keep silent, "do you not know, Madame, that there is in the world a secret society one could call the company of 'melancholics'? They are people who have differed from others since their birth; their hearts are larger, and their blood flows more rapidly; they wish and desire more; they breathe with more ardor, and their passions are more violent, more burning than those of the common run of men. . . . Only, they are searching the tree of life for flowers that the others do not even suspect exist, flowers hidden beneath the dead leaves and withered boughs. What do the others know of the voluptuous pleasure of sadness or despair? . . ."*

"*But why,*" *asked Marie, turning away her eyes indifferently, "why do you call them the 'melancholics' when, in fact, they think only of life's joys and pleasures, and not of its harshness and pain?*"

"*Why?*" *he cried in a tone of impatience and disdain. "Because every earthly joy is brief and perishable, false and imperfect; because voluptuous delight, no sooner has it blossomed like a rose, sheds its leaves like a tree in autumn; because each of life's superb pleasures, in fullest flower and resplendent with beauty, on the very brink of taking hold of you, is gnawed by a cancer, so that you sense, from the moment it comes near your lips, its rattle of decay . . . And you ask why I call them the 'melancholics,' when every shiver of exaltation is but joy's last anguished sigh, when all beauty is beauty that deceives; all happiness, happiness that's dashed.*"

JENS PETER JACOBSEN,
Marie Grubbe

Introduction

EVER SINCE CLASSICAL ANTIQUITY philosophers have considered melancholia a constitutive part of being. The fact that they even felt the need to construct a cosmogony[1] to argue for its existence should come as no surprise to us. For the Ancients this ailment afflicting all human beings was worthy of astral projection. Their inscribing it into the order of stellar and planetary motion is proof that even if all humans are not directly stricken with "Saturn's sickness," all are likely, by some conjunction or other, to encounter the black sorrow, the paralyzing horror known as "melancholia."

"Black bile sickness"—for such is the etymology of the melancholic disorder—conjures up that primal mourning I myself have come to consider a founding moment for subjectivity.[2]

Here it is important to recall Freud's text "Mourning and Melancholia." Dated 1917, it was actually written in 1915 in the wake of Karl Abraham's paper "Preliminaries to the Investigation and

---

[1] Cf. Plutarque, *Du visage qui apparaît dans le rond de la lune* [Of the Face That Appears in the Circle of the Moon], critical edition, trans. and commentaries P. Raingeau (Paris: Les Belles Lettres, 1935). Erwin Panofsky, Fritz Saxe, and Raymond Khibansky, *Saturn & Melancholy: Studies in the History of Philosophy, Religion and Art* (London, 1964). Aristotle, *Les Problèmes* [Problems], trans. B. St. Hilaire (Paris, 1991), vol. II, sect. xxx. Jean Starobinski, "Histoire du traitement de la mélancholie des origines à 1900" ["History of the Treatment of Melancholy from Earliest Times to 1900"], in *Acte psychosomatique*, no. 3, 1960, cited by Maxime Préaud in *Mélancholies*, Format/Art coll. (Paris: Éditions Herscher, 1982).

[2] Cf. my working hypothesis on the dead child in my *Fragments de langue maternelle* [Fragments of Mother Tongue] (Paris: Payot, 1979). 2d ed. (Point Hors Ligne, 1993).

Psychoanalytic Treatment of Manic-Depressive Madness and Related States," which was presented at the Third Congress of Psychoanalysis on September 11, 1911. Freud's contribution would in turn prompt another text by Karl Abraham, dated 1924, "Manic-Depressive States and Pregenital Organizational Stages of the Libido"; it serves as the introduction to "An Outline of the History of Libidinal Development, Based on the Psychoanalysis of Mental Disorders."

Today it is a foregone conclusion that Freud was inspired by Karl Abraham. In fact, in a letter dated May 4, 1915, he writes to his pupil:

> Your observations on melancholia were very valuable to me; I have unscrupulously drawn from it all that seemed useful to me to put into my essay. Above all I have benefited from your remarks on the oral phase of the libido; likewise I have referred to the link that you establish with mourning. I was, however, spared the pains of offering the harsh criticism you ask of me, since almost everything you wrote was to my liking. I would only underscore two points: on the one hand, you do not sufficiently clarify what is essential to your hypothesis, namely, its topical aspect, the regression of the libido and the lifting of the investment of the unconscious object; on the other hand, you place greatest emphasis on sadism and anal eroticism. . . . Anal eroticism, the castration complex, etc. are ubiquitous sources of excitation, and as such, they form an integral part of *every* pathological syndrome. . . . the explanation of this disorder can be provided only by considering its workings from a *dynamical, topical,* and *economical* point of view.[3]

Thus, as with Abraham's hypotheses on Akhnaton, Freud plunders his Berlin disciple, all the while upbraiding him. In essence, he tells him he's going to make use of his discoveries, but hastens to caution him not to reduce melancholia to just any pathological syndrome by making reference to a ubiquitous source of excitation.

Beyond the glimpse this letter provides into the sort of ties Freud

---

[3] Sigmund Freud and Karl Abraham, *Correspondence 1907–1926*, trans. F. Cambon and J. P. Grosein (Paris: Gallimard, 1969), 224–225.

established with his students and contemporaries, it helps us to understand that working out a theory of melancholia would mark a turning point in Freud's work. In the monument psychoanalysis was becoming, melancholia would demand pride of place if it were not to risk being viewed in debased fashion as one nosographical category among others.

And let's not forget here that "Mourning and Melancholia" comes after "On Narcissism: An Introduction" and "Instincts and Their Vicissitudes," and four years before *Beyond the Pleasure Principle*. This fundamental text, which Freud spent a year working out (spring 1919–May 1920), cannot fail to give a new dimension to his theory of melancholia. The introduction of the death drive and its connection to the *erotic* drives allow Freud and his successors a new approach to this disorder. It will henceforth be understood as a structural element of the subject, marking the impossibility of carrying out the mourning process for an object. This inability to mourn marks the unbinding of drives that lies at the very core of melancholic destruction.

Finally let us point out that in "Reflections upon War and Death,"[4] a text contemporary—is it any coincidence?—with "Mourning and Melancholia," Freud wrote:

> Our unconscious is just as inaccessible to the idea of our own death, as murderously minded toward the stranger, as divided or ambivalent towards the loved, as was man in earliest antiquity. But how far we have moved from this primitive state in our conventionally civilized attitude toward death! . . .
>
> [O]ur unconscious will murder even for trifles; like the ancient Athenian law of Draco, it knows no other punishment for crime than death; and this has a certain consistency, for even injury to our almighty and autocratic ego is at bottom a crime of *lèse-majesté*. And so, if we are to be judged by the wishes in our unconscious, we are, like primitive man, simply a gang of murderers. . . .

---

4 Sigmund Freud, "Reflections upon War and Death" (1915), trans. E. Colburn Mayne, reprinted in *Character and Culture* (New York: Collier Books, 1963), 107–133.

With the exception of only a very few situations, there adheres to the tenderest and closest of our affections a vestige of hostility which can excite an unconscious death-wish. . . . . Is it not for us to confess that in our civilized attitude towards death we are once more living psychologically beyond our means, and must reform and give truth its due? Would it not be better to give death the place in actuality and in our thoughts which properly belongs to it, and to yield a little more prominence to that unconscious attitude toward death which we have hitherto so carefully suppressed? . . . To endure life remains, when all is said, the first duty of all living beings. Illusion can have no value if it makes this more difficult for us. We remember the old saying: *Si vis pacem, para bellum*. If you desire peace, prepare for war.

It would be timely thus to paraphrase it: *Si vis vitam, para mortem*. If you would endure life, be prepared for death.

But what might this regression be to which Freud refers? To understand it better, we must go back to the chapter "Our Attitude Towards Death":

It was then but consistent to extend life backward into the past, to conceive of former existences, transmigrations of the soul and reincarnation, all with the purpose of depriving death of its meaning as the termination of life. So early did the denial of death, which above we designated a convention of civilization, actually originate.[5]

Remarkably enough, this text is an expurgated if not censored version of a lecture Freud gave to the Vienna B'nai B'rith lodge on February 6, 1915.[6] In this talk, which gives us an idea of the breadth of Freud's Jewish cultural background, the last sentence quoted above is replaced by a passage of great interest to us on several counts:

---

[5] Sigmund Freud, "Reflections upon War and Death," 128.

[6] The text of this lecture came to me in its Spanish version (Sigmund Freud, "Nosotros y la muerte," trans. A. Ackermann Pilari, *Freudiana*, no. 1, ed. Paidos, Catalonia, 1991) via Daniel Koren, who translated it into French on the occasion of a lecture that I gave to the Paris Arbeiter-Ring [Bund] in 1990. The first version of the *Moses* [Moses and Monotheism] had also been presented to this same B'nai B'rith lodge, which seems to have been the place where Freud presented his most problematic and most fruitful texts.

It is highly significant that our Holy Scriptures did not place value upon this necessity for man to be vouchsafed continued existence beyond death. On the contrary, we read in certain instances: "Only the living praise God."[7] I assume—and surely you know more than I on this point—that the popular Jewish religion and the literature that comes after the Holy Scriptures hold a different opinion on the doctrine of immortality. Yet I would also like to include this point among the factors that made it impossible for the Jewish religion to take the place of other religions when theirs entered their waning days.[8]

This worldview that Freud adopts does not strike me as alien to the findings of *Beyond the Pleasure Principle* and the discovery of the binding of drives that links death to the living. This theoretical advance manages to deny the subject any consolation projecting toward a future that would guarantee a divinity, be it one absolutely transcendental or, on the contrary, immanent, dead, and resurrected.

Such a position relates to narcissism; it views death not with the melancholic's eyes, which glimpse the workings of decay in the very midst of life,[9] but by admitting that there is no other *beyond* but *beyond the pleasure principle.* It follows the Freudian postulate that there is no representation of death in the unconscious. Consequently, death is present in the living, but as a drive whose binding with the partial (or so-called erotic) drives assumes that desire, and

---

7 [Psalm 115:118. According to the King James Version, the verse reads: "The dead praise not the LORD, neither any that go down into silence." Trans.]

8 Here Freud adopts a position that, from the Sadducees to Maimonides, was one of rationalistic (and aristocratic) Jewish thought. Beyond death lies the unknowable. The abandonment of this absence of assurance by other religions (Christian and Islamic) in adopting notions of Paradise and Hell (which a certain popular and pietistic Judaism also took up) in fact contributed to their popularity among the Gentiles, whereas Judaism, by excluding these notions, isolated itself from the vast majority's delusions. In so doing, it failed to "cash in."

9 A position that the Desert Fathers of Egypt (for instance, Macarius the Coptic or [Saint] Mary of Egypt) and certain Jewish mystics of the seventeenth century (Isaac Luria, Moses Cordovero, or Chaim Vital Calabrese) shared. Cf. Jacques Hassoun, *Les Passions intraitables* [Untreatable Passions] (Paris: Aubier, 1993).

what causes it, structurally represents an operation deducible from the death drive's inscription in the Ego.

As such, melancholia for Freud is a malady of the Ego, occurring precisely where the death drive is inscribed.

We can say, then, that the melancholic position represents "a regression in history"[10] only if we consider that the living need to be consoled for not being immortal.[11]

These considerations lead us back to our relation to bereavement, to loss, and to death: for if the partial drives and the death drive are constantly at work on the living being, if the work of mourning following the demise of someone close to us—or the collapse of a set of ideals—is characteristic of a living person, then melancholia is an effect of a disconnection of drives. This unbinding of drives reveals that conditions had always been combined to transform loss into an enigma, plunging the subject into the infinite sorrow of an impossible bereavement.

Among the maladies of bereavement, we will encounter passion in its funereal aspect, which Lacan has designated by the obsolete term of *mourre*[12]: it is like the ruse that the death drive adopts in

---

[10] Let us recall at this juncture that Lacan, in his seminar on *L'éthique de la psychanalyse* [*The Ethics of Psychoanalysis*] (Paris: Le Seuil, 1986), 248, links history to the activity of the drive(s): "The actual drive . . . cannot be reduced to the complexity of the tendency understood in its broadest sense, the sense of the energetic. It contains a historical dimension whose true import we must point out. This dimension is marked by the insistence with which it presents itself, insofar as it relates to something memorable in having been memorized. The memorizing, the historicization, is coextensive with the functioning of the drive in what is called the human psyche. It is also there that destruction is registered, that it enters into the register of experience."

[11] In this case, one would have to be "the hero who does not believe in his own death," as Freud writes, or else be that person whose voiding forbids him to believe in his own life, and who lingers on in a state of rottenness, neither mortal nor immortal, content to survive in apathy and immobility.

[12] Many Lacanians have considered the term *la mourre* as a coupling of *l'amour* [love] and *la mort* [death] . . . reason enough for them to grant it a considerable theoretical importance. The Littré dictionary gives the following definition for *la mourre*: "a game imported from Italy, which consists of quickly brandishing one's fist showing some fingers raised and the others closed, so that the other person has to guess how many one is holding up."

order to bind itself to the other so-called conversion drives of the species/individual/libido.

Melancholic passion is a moment of the sudden surfacing of a phenomenal object that is the cause of all desires, an object that will mold itself onto some chosen being whose appearance captivates the subject and draws it into an experience of radical desubjectivization; and it is addressed to the Ego it so affects.

Isn't the other with whom the melancholic will fall in love similar to that Ideal Ego which Narcissus, racked with the absence of an(y) image, loved to the point of death? If falling in love can sometimes end in a love story in which desire wins back its rights, it may also prove to be just like melancholy in the way it disconnects drives. As we'll see, the melancholic's suffering attests to the unwitting knowledge of guilt that can be linked to a murder forever deferred. Isn't this what sinks melancholics into their remarkable passivity, into an infinite bereavement that reduces every word to an endless complaint heavily fraught with self-accusations?

Let us recall here that for Karl Abraham the passivity characteristic of melancholics is often triggered by some overwhelming situation that renders them incapable of reacting to the event.

Social and institutional life offer us many examples: anything that makes citizens passive inevitably entails the sort of withdrawal of object investments typical of melancholics. Confronted with the enigma that the Other's violence poses, the subject—here brought to subjection—finds himself somehow confronted with an absence of otherness. Where all the components of the social bond should be—audible, comprehensible—suddenly what looms up instead is a surprise that can only alienate the subject. This loss of moorings—and the disconnection it creates—stems from a fierceness the other takes on, striking the subject like some painful memory, the indefinable feeling of a loss that plummets him into suffering, a sense of worthlessness, inhibition, and passivity. Throughout his life Freud evoked this passivity, this appeal to tyranny, marveling that these dimensions could emerge from the social bond itself.

The introduction of the death drive—Freud's most metapsychological act of theoretical trail-blazing, with the greatest implications for civilization—has enabled us to understand the melancholy *jouissance* of those who pay exorbitant tribute to *le Mal* [Evil] making themselves henchmen or agents in the dirty-work of various führers, those supreme guides or theoretical geniuses of times past, present, or to come.

But isn't this, after all, what prompted Thomas Mann to declare, on the occasion of Freud's eightieth birthday: "Psychoanalysis is a form of melancholy knowledge"? Did he mean by this that the psychoanalyst is one who never stops shedding illusions? That psychoanalysis is constitutionally unable to issue a how-to manual for living, attempting rather to understand the discontents with which civilization is confronted? So we would like to think, in any case.

Chapter 1

Janus the Melancholic

It would be a gross illusion to search physiology for the instinctive basis of these rules, more in keeping with nature, that the ideal of the most advanced cultures imposes on weaning, as it does on the whole set of mores. In fact, weaning, by one of those operational contingencies it entails, is often a psychic trauma whose individual effects, so-called mental anorexias, oral drug addictions, gastric neuroses, reveal their cause to psychoanalysis.

> JACQUES LACAN, *Les Complexes
> familiaux dans la formation de
> l'individu* [The Family
> Complexes in the Forming of
> the Individual] (Paris: Navarin,
> 1984)

HE PHONES ME, anxious-sounding and a little breathless; his words come hurtling out, as though struggling to keep pace with some thought that's trapped in some as yet unfathomable drama. There's too much urgency in his voice. I ask him to call me back tomorrow, not really expecting that he will: tension this high rarely can stand the wait. But he does call back and shows up for his appointment at the time we've set.

Twenty-eight years old, slim, slight but surprisingly sturdy-looking, with dark, darting eyes, and pale, almost translucent skin, meticulously groomed, he describes his suffering and his anxiety in a staccato. He seems ready to implode at any moment. Yet for all its intense agitation, there's something immobile and stalled about his talk: at times he seems to buckle and cave in, to go limp, not like a rag doll, but more like a muscle twitching with tetanus, its spasms increased by physical pain.

For ten years he was heavily addicted to heroin: to get it, he cheated, lied, stole—stole a lot—though always sticking to certain rules that kept him from ever being caught and charged. He experienced devastating romantic passions in a body all desire had fled. He's been off heroin for two years. He's gone back to the university, finished his studies quite successfully, taken a job, and been highly valued by his employers.

Whereas he had managed to wean himself from heroin, he was still addicted to various surrogate drugs, though well aware of their harmfulness. He was eager to understand all that had happened to him.

All past attempts to commit himself to an analysis had broken off quite abruptly. This time he was determined to stick with it—and the only reason for that was apparently that my immediate request that he "call back tomorrow" established a distance that had, unwittingly on my part, struck just the right note.

Let me cite some basic components of the history of this young man I'll call Janus: born in a village near Lyon, he grew up very much on his own, despite having a number of siblings, in the back of his parents' shop; few remarkable events emerge from the dullness of a childhood focused totally on his excellent performance in school. One fact, however, does stand out against the deadly monotony: when his mother brings another child into the world, the twelve-year-old Janus is forced to turn his room over to his little sister. Overnight, it's as though he's lost face, been thrown into exile far from his immediate family, in the outbuildings of his grandparents' farm, which is actually quite close. For a long time this fact—which I regarded as a screen memory—was something of a riddle. It seems to have marked a turning point in his history, yet one still blank, uninscribed.

In attempting to represent this event, we might envision some sort of mnemic enclave, a twilit no-man's-land, or view it perhaps as we would those molecular crystals whose only partially attainable dissolution gives the liquid in question an undefinable opacity: since, for all its apparent clarity such opacity signals the presence of a body similar in nature to the solution, yet so incongruous, it can be perceived only as mysterious and displaced. The event, neither repressed nor denied, is all too conspicuously present. This indiscreet presence is grounds for a quasi-legal "case" the subject will— short of clearing it up—defend to the death.

Only twice did Janus mention this incident, as though, both belonging *and* not belonging to his history, it gave his existence a style, keeping him from another lapse into heroin: he needed to go on living his damaged existence in the hope of finding out the real story.

Before entering analysis, he had never overcome this hesitancy. Which is to say, he still occupied the sites of this event: his wanderings brought him back to them, all his sorry drifting led him to rediscover the path to that little room where he had been abandoned. This enclosure he remained so passionately attached to, like some prisoner to his cell, is the place of a confinement that shuts him out from life.

Being of Absence

How can we think about drug users without confronting the difficulty we encounter in using the complex phenomenon known as *addiction* to define what clearly destroys, damages, and yet effectively prolongs the mere pretext of a life? Is there a psychic structure that can account for this quite peculiar *appétance* [craving]—this predilection whose first name could well be said to be Urgency, and family name, *Jouissance*? Any drug that becomes necessary on a daily basis is not the stuff of desire but rather of despair (or of need).

In *Opium* Jean Cocteau writes:

Let us profit from insomnia to attempt the impossible: to describe the craving.

Byron said: "Love cannot withstand seasickness." Like love, like seasickness, the craving penetrates everywhere. Resistance is useless. At first a malaise, then things become worse. Imagine a silence equivalent to the crying of thousands of children whose mothers do not return to give them the breast. The lover's anxiety transposed into nervous awareness. An absence which dominates, a negative despotism. . . .

Your body was waiting only for a sign. One pipe is enough.[1]

What might this negative despotism be? What inner tyrant is this to whom the subject submits first with delight, then with horror, and finally with glum indifference? What tyrant but that of an absence erected into a being, one which rules the subject's entire existence? For this reason we can venture the hypothesis that the drug takes the place of an enigmatic absence that continually, compulsively manifests itself. However, this absence that torments the addicted subject will not be replaced by the drug. The drug comes, as it were, in the nick of time to attempt, paradoxically, to release the subject from the enigma of an absence, by endowing that absence with the solidity of an object (the drug), which the subject will then erect into a being of absence. The subject knows neither what nor whom he has lost. That's the impossibility he faces. This twofold condition tends to cancel out the loss which, though missing from the signifying series, is no less tyrannically present. From this point on, before presenting himself as waste product—as wreckage, rubbish, scrap—the drug user elevates the status of waste itself, making it seem the only conceivable cause of his desire.

A person in a state of addiction is not shit, but takes shit—so-called—to feel first like a king, and then ultimately to merge totally with what he puts into his body: at some moment in this process, he's made of shit and considers himself as such.

---

[1] Jean Cocteau, *Opium, The Diary of a Cure*, trans. Margaret Crosland and Sinclair Road (New York: Grove Press, 1958), 23.

This is why I'm suggesting that it is not death the addicted subject aspires to, but rot, trash, the remainder in the Lacanian sense of the term. It is also an identification with what he is waiting for that will make him the vassal of a pure, desperately sought-after expectancy. In these conditions the drug becomes the pretext for creating expectation in the very place of an absent signifier (loss)—one which has never yet manifested itself to the subject.

Let us recall here that the remainder, or what Lacan calls *objet petit a,* enters into the formation of our Ideal Ego as a separate part outside the mirroring process, able as such to give form and outline to the mirror image. Now, for someone enslaved to heroin, a part of this remainder, which constitutes us as a subject in our relation to the other, would seem to be singularly absent.

Whence the need to summon this remainder into being in the only register still available: the Real. Everything happens as though the operation taking place at the mirror stage had miscarried on the level of one of the avatars of the object. We might translate this failure by saying that the murder of the Thing [*das Ding*[2]] has not been fully carried out. To grasp this statement, we must refer to the hypothesis Freud advances in *Beyond the Pleasure Principle:* A living being's structure is dominated by the pleasure/unpleasure principle, a principle of homeostasis which regulates its relations with the outer world with a view toward reducing tensions. Thus, for the speaking being, there must exist an active authority that tries to fend off anything, from either the outer or the inner world, that would create too much tension. It is only "highlights" of subjectivized reality that human beings come into contact with. Moreover, the Thing will be from the outset that which is isolated, external. It is what is "radically foreign," unassimilable. Foreign, alien (Lacan designates it as an absence, if not a hole), this Thing will be able to function for the subject as a reference. It will be the primordial object, lost forever, yet in a certain sense never entirely lost, since it

---

2 Jacques Lacan discusses the *Thing* particularly in his seminar *"L'éthique de la psychan- alyse"* (Paris: Le Seuil, 1986), chap. IV and V.

is always something to re-find. As such, it could be considered a reference enabling the subject to gauge what is incomparable in his desire. Now, the pleasure principle that governs the quest for this object always keeps it at a distance. The objects of satisfaction, the objects of the drive are not the Thing, but rather decoys, place-holders.

Here Lacan recalls that if the fundamental law of humanity is the prohibition of incest, this law, in the very act of being articulated, shows that the incestuous desire it forbids is the most basic of desires. This is why the Thing can be said to represent the primal, archaic mother, the mother who is the goal of incest.

Once distance has been established from this primal object, the fulfillment of incestuous desire, experienced as forbidden, in fact becomes impossible. The impossible aspect of incestuous *jouissance* with the mother is the very condition for the survival of speech. Distance from the Thing is the very condition for the existence of the speaking subject—what Lacan calls the *parlêtre* [this being, *l'être, "par lettre," "*by the letter." Trans.]. Lacan can thus posit that the symbol, the symbolic, is tantamount to the murder of the Thing.

This set of hypotheses enables us to give a new dimension to the Thing, starting with the object's place in sublimation: the object of desire always bears the mark of its narcissistic origin, embellished by elaborations that are imaginary yet fit for social valorization, cultural recognition, notably in the realm of art. Indeed, sublimation does not consist of "changing object" but of "changing goal." It tends to elevate the object to the dignity of the Thing, to the dignity of what, being beyond comparison, is also revealed as an absence. Yet how can one part of the psychic object—or its avatars—be represented in this way in the Real precisely when we are presenting the object as riddled with decay, or otherwise lacking?

Perhaps the example of a lover's passion might provide some means of response to this question. For such is the paradox sur-rounding the thunderbolt that is passion: brutally, with nothing that would seem to indicate the possibility of an encounter between this woman and that man, passion suddenly brings them together—and alienates them from each other. In a split second, it springs from the mere image of the woman who reveals a passion she is unaware of having roused. This dazzlement, this body-kindling heat, and numbing chill, might best be called the *flash*.

So it is in the manner of passion that the drug user is led to recognize in the drug-object what has always been lacking and represents the cause of his rapture. It has always stood for an absence, has always been waited for. . . . But from this moment on, absence, the wait, the inaugural (but not "founding") astonishment, will make up that deadly ensemble that collapses together the terms that fill in for the object's non-arrival, a no-show of that part of the object that lacks the function of lost object.

Henceforth, we must understand the encounter with this "heroin(e) of olden days" (which might be the most adequate nickname for drugs in their entirety) as the attempt to summon the object into being where before there was nothing—a way, like any other, to lift yourself out of a horrible solitude that no so-called transitional object (security blanket, thumb, or nipple) has ever yet come to embody or represent.

Thus, the drug as the inert agent of a devouring passion or an iron-clad, intractable figure,[3] crystallizes and indexes a very old form of melancholia, one contemporary with the mirror stage, which had remained unknown to the subject and those closest to him. In this regard the drug would fulfill a function as origin. Now, if we are willing to consider that discourse, language, the signifying chain work upon the subject all his life, we may say that this is "original" only insofar as some discursive fragment that had been absent, or had failed to achieve symbolization, presents itself now in a dusky Real in the guise of a *primum movens* [prime mover].

We can, then, understand how the heroin(e)-drug, be-all and

---

[3] As one says of a dominatrix, for such is the implicit demand formulated by the man who offers himself to her as an object.

end-all of an alienated existence, can prompt those cosmic distortions that make someone prey to this waste process at once a poor beggar and an omnipotent god. As Cocteau writes of the pangs of need:

> The symptoms of the craving are of so strange a kind that they cannot be described. Only the nurses in clinics succeed in forming some impression. (The symptoms do not differ from serious ones). Imagine that the earth is turning a little less fast, that the moon is coming a little closer. . . . One always speaks of the slavery of opium. The regularity it imposes on the passing hours is not only a discipline, it is also a liberation.[4]

This liberation that "emasculates the smoker" (the verb is Cocteau's) takes place for the sake of that "exacting mistress" who tolerates no competition, no intervention but her own, in the existence of whoever has set her up as tyrant. At this point, we realize, then, that the object we call a drug is established by the said addict or "toxicomaniac"[5] in place of what immediately departed [from his life].

We call this a drug, though we could certainly find other names. Allen Ginsberg, William Burroughs, Jack Kerouac, the American counterculture, Robert Lapassade, and many others have tried to define this elusive substance whose names are legion. From "the white queen" to "shit," its designation runs the gamut of a rapture, a mad delight [jouissance] in which its prey loses all—face included— in the attempt to form the missing fragment of an image.

Janus the Melancholic: so we have dubbed him. The formulation is in itself paradoxical if we're willing to consider that Janus the inventor of money and of navigation, the civilizer of Latium, the peaceful legislator, had two faces. Now, a person in thrall to a drug

---

4 Jean Cocteau, *Opium, The Diary of a Cure,* 56 and 53.

5 And not the other way around, as sociopolitical discourse or traditional medicine would have it.

loses the face that looks toward the future and never ceases to contemplate a past whose very outline he can hardly make out. Being amputated from that part that allows him to consider the future, he is expelled from the civil, the political, order, from the City; as a result, he is no more than a suffering body, craving whatever might pull him out of an infinite sadness. Janus says:

When I first took heroin, it didn't do anything to me, at the worst it made me throw up; then I kept shooting up, once, twice a day, but I could still stop any time. If I did miss a day of shooting up, I'd just be swamped with this endless feeling of sadness I couldn't explain; I had no idea where it could have come from. What it made me think of? I guess of my mother, who never noticed anything about our bodies except our pain, before we'd even made the slightest complaint about it.

And even today, day after day, through ersatz drugs, Janus takes care of this body that has no existence apart from its suffering. Like Narcissus in Ovid,[6] he contemplates the absence of his body and convinces himself of his existence by taking a succession of surrogate substances that fill in for the now-abandoned object-drug.

In the absence of mourning, and by taking the place of melancholia—in its classic form—the drug, from its initial flash to the final dependency, offers itself up as a third term of identity. Along with the most dramatic of running sores, loose teeth, thin hair, skeletal thinness, abscesses, comes a hollowing out of the body that gives way only to "eyes without a face," eyes that contemplate the reflection of a suffering staged and enacted on a daily basis: the internal image of this body "did not take," never congealed. Couldn't we consider that it's in the mythic time of the first form of identification—the one of so-called incorporation of the father— that the *infans,* this unspeaking child, was put in the impossible situation of being offered a first identification, one able to give solidity to a psychic trace of the mirror image? This impossible

---

6 Cf. F.-R. Ingold, "La dépendance," in "Drogue et société," *Esprit,* November-December 1980.

situation would be the premise for an impairment of identification with the father, whose function it is to uphold the Law, leaving a hole, a gaping that would make the *infans* a being in whom the only thing that can apparently create a limit is this lethal, ultimate object, which as *omnipotentia supplex* [humbly entreating omnipotence][7] continually beckons: the drug. From now on, this failure of the first form of identification, linked to the object's absence—in its function as lost object—could account (at least in my hypothesis) for this particular form of melancholia whereby cruelty is unleashed and marginality instated in place of the law.

If we're willing to consider, then, that the inscription of the death drive in the Ego, which requires a double operation (incorporation of the father and assumption of the mirror image, set against the object's loss) is revealed here to be impaired, we realize that the cruelty with which the drug is treated represents an attempt to establish what failed to occur on the part of the paternal function.

This absence of object (which, in Janus's case, came to constitute a trauma at the second stage, contemporary with the event represented by the episode of having to give up the room) might be termed a failure in weaning. It certainly illustrates Lacan's statement that death is the object of an appetite. It also follows the outline of the nostalgia Lacan relates to the "metaphysical mirage of universal harmony, the mystic gulf of affective fusion, [the] social utopia of a totalitarian overseeing, all of which issue from the obsession with a lost prenatal paradise and the darkest aspiration for death."[8]

From this various propositions follow that may account for the drama experienced by one addicted to an object-drug:

- the instatement of the object-drug in place of the internal object he was unable to mourn;

---

[7] Saint Bernard's name for the Virgin Mary.

[8] Lacan, "Les Complexes familiaux dans la formation de l'individu," in *Encyclopédie française*, Vol. VIII, s.v. "Le complexe du sevrage" [The Weaning Complex] (1938; reprint, Paris: Éditions Navarin, 1984), 35.

- cruelty exerted upon his own body, in the wake of a failed encounter with whatever would have had the effect of setting itself up as the Law;

- finally, eclipse of a (first) identification, which finds itself being supplanted by the identity which the social order throws back upon him, and which he takes up and displays like some choice piece of butcher's meat: "I am a drug addict."

This identity, "I'm a junkie," is more static than ecstatic in expression. It's the index of a foundering, a wreckage of subjectivity, of a last effort to say "I" instead of some more indefinite pronoun. This "world of its own"[9] that the drug creates is that in which the subject de-nominates (i.e., names but un-names) himself, that in which the City, by being hateful, ceases to be a City for the drug taker; now it represents only the place from which incomprehensible edicts are issued.[10] If the drug user considers that society is governed by arbitrariness, we may then ask ourselves a question that entails our responsibility as social subjects and as citizens: "Why today? What is it, in the society of the last twenty years, that has allowed for the mass spread of drugs?"

We know the answer: Long the sole property of aesthetes and intellectuals on the one hand, and ex-colonials on the other, before joining the panoply first of the American, then of the West European counterculture, drugs have, for about the last dozen years, become an object of common currency, with their own language, their established buying and selling areas in the poorer quarters of Paris, in workers' suburbs (or should we say ex-workers?)—in that devastated, destroyed, apocalyptic part of the city embodying a space on which are writ large both *no future* and *apocalypse now*: two formulas that bracket time, make Janus lose face, and acknowledge only the instant.

---

9 Olivier Mongin, "L'esprit de la loi dans les sociétés modernes, culpabilité ou responsabilité," *Esprit,* 148.

10 Reference to Catherine Trautman, statement on commemoration of fiftieth anniversary of the destruction of Strasbourg's synagogue by the Nazis: "A city in which racism and anti-Semitism prevail is not a hateful city: it ceases to be a city at all."

Meaning, the instant of unbearable waiting? the instant of the flash? The infinite instant of the child who, having lost his transitional object, finds himself naked, abandoned, and defenseless? The instant in which the child flees sudden, inexplicable death? The twilit instant in which vision is beclouded, the images bent out of shape, peopled with ghosts and hallucinations of absence? I myself tend to consider that the drug-object is one of the figures for the linkage that articulates Evil, *le Mal,* as it works upon the social, breeding individual unhappiness [*malheur*] and melancholy cruelty.

Evil, Unhappiness, and the Denial of History

Evil, ill and illness, woe and want—all that is contained in the French word *le Mal*—can be said to be an inheritance constituted and structured in the social by one scandalous pronouncement: if the Other exists, it is only as the other of suffering and exclusion, the bearer of an untenable, uniquely untraceable difference.

Any city that claims to have reached a state of homogenization can only shortchange and debase the Other. But what is a society that denies otherness but a mere horde, all the more savage, all the more melancholic, in being made-up, cosmetically disguised, dolled up in drag through a set of decadent institutions designed to flaunt a discourse of consensus? What's a modernity divested of symbolized differentiation and the social tensions that represent it, but one which finds its bonds coming undone, so that it can now only conceive of the Other as endowed with traits of suffering?

Such societies are forgetful of their history and their past investments. They burn what they once worshipped; they preach the lie in the name of a truth they deny.

To give one example: Stalinism for the working class (and those who grant themselves the right to speak in its name) represented for a half-century the *Truth* (in Russian, *Pravda*) and the least blame cast on Stalin's regime was considered treason. With its fall, Stalinism dragged down a whole set of other elements directly related to the laws of the City's functioning; that destitution, the disappointment that reveals lying and denial leaves, instead of hope for a brighter future, despair. The societies that flee tension where it arises—at the heart of the City—shift the question onto the plane of the individual.

Another example will clarify my argument: it concerns what so brutally afflicts those black Americans who are, at the present moment, apparently being decimated by heroin and crack. Shut out from American society, the blacks are identified with the throwaway part, the rot, of the American dream.[11] This identification of Afro-Americans in their entirety with a designation has become, strictly speaking, their distinguishing, if not their rallying, sign—against the background of a political wasteland and the ideological simulacra they cling to, isn't this entire group located at the very intersection of *Mal* and *malheur,* Evil and wretchedness? Drugs represent, in certain cases, the reified object that permits the redemption of an injured symbolic identification. So it is that the ill that stems from subjectivity can at times be trapped in the vise of a historical event.

Confronted with Evil, the subject seems to have no other recourse but to attack the person he invests with all the trappings of a ruthless puppeteer: whence his quest for a cruelty to practice on his own body, in the name of a mendacious history consonant with the subject's own history, when he finds himself confronted with a new truth (the Orwellian scenario par excellence[12]) that has collapsed into other lies, other exclusions, other striking absences. This resonance between the historical and the subjective, which has all the pernicious effects of a passion, is destructive and lethal. It can establish the other as marginal, as a cast-off, as a skinhead, a stormtrooper, carrier of some blind, absolute violence unleashed in the name of an omnipotent master, the guarantor of the horde's cohesion.

---

[11] Cf. Spike Lee film, *Do the Right Thing* (1989).

[12] Let us recall that in his work *1984,* George Orwell describes a totalitarian society that alters its history and its truth on a day-to-day basis.

Should it surprise us, then, that in the countries of Eastern Europe, which have attempted to erase history—unchristening their cities, bargaining away their pasts without taking stock of the monstrous errors that have tainted them—that we should witness the appearance on an epidemic scale of unprecedented outbreaks of violence in the name of ethnicity? Should it surprise us to see these same regions overrun (after a period in which they were relatively spared) by the drug-object and by drugs?

Drugs, in any event, have a bright future before them, given the quite unfortuitous conjunction that reigns today between political despair, mourning for ideologies and political commitment, melancholy born out of the collapse of social reference points, and the subjective problematic of those once subjugated to Stalin's *Janus,* a two-faced god at once blood-suffused and bovine. Acknowledging this prospect does not mean giving in to pessimism but merely being realistic. And this period—with its seemingly triumphant bracketing of history[13] and its denial—is the one that has produced a negationism if not a negativism capable of replacing one cruelty with another still greater.

But to conclude here, I think it's necessary to keep the veil lifted a moment longer on Janus and shed a bit more light on what might have clinched his decision to stay with analysis.

In that first phone call of his, when I asked him to call back, my intent was to introduce the time-signifier ("till tomorrow"), which could only lead him to relativize his devouring wait; in ceasing to represent an existential project, this waiting necessarily became an element in the very rhythm of the analysis.

For if it's true that the analyst's work tends to give solidity to some internal object, in the treatments of people who are addicts or adepts of some drug-object, this need is presented categorically.

---

13 It is thus that the former Soviet Union attempted to *do* as *if* the period that extends from 1917 to 1922 was a black hole, whereas the "ex-people's democracies" tend somewhat to dream of a pre-1945 restoration of order, all the while sinking into ethnicidal delirium.

On the one hand, the transference, as the formation-site for this object, by altering the time of the infinite wait through both the rhythm and regularity of sessions, and the contract that is its guarantee, introduces the subject to the symbolic order. From that point on it is a matter of conveying and interpreting the drug to be the object the analysand has had to set up in place of what would have allowed him to represent his melancholy prostration. The knowledge constituted in the transference tends to allow the subject to mourn, and from this mourning reconstitute the (previously ever-absent) internal object that should have been his support.

To replace naked, enigmatic pain by the work of mourning, mourning, that is, for an object or an abstraction set up in its place[14]—that is our task.

An analysand, in other words, should be able to measure the time that separates one session from another, sense the analyst's own subjection to this session time and rhythm, include this in the framework of existence, and be able to understand the universality of the Law, construct the object that is able to give back shape and form to an absent image, reintroducing it into the course of his history, and begin at last to think about this passion whose object is an endless wait: this passion the drug rouses.

---

[14] Freud, in "Mourning and Melancholia," cites those abstractions such as political ideals, patriotism, liberty, that are apt to replace the object.

Chapter 2

"From one passion to the other"

PASSION ARISES out of a chance encounter, always asymmetrical. One person is held captive by a detail that will—for a time—condense all causes of desire. As Saint John of the Cross exclaims:

> *You stared at that one lock*
> *of windblown hair you saw against*
> *my nape, and on my neck*
> *you were a prisoner*
> *gashing yourself in one of my eyes.*[1]

The impassioned person, a captive of the movement of a hand or a glance, will find himself riveted to what impassions him, to that convulsive beauty, "erotic-and-veiled, exploding-and-fixed, magical-and-adverbial" that André Breton evokes in *L'Amour fou* [Mad Love].[2]

It is rare, indeed exceptional, for the impassioned person, in the period of exaltation or ecstatic bliss that seems to characterize him, to feel the need to request analysis. It's at the moment when time is

---

[1] "Cantico Espiritual" [Spiritual Canticle], 1st redaction, codex of Sanlucar de Barrameda, in *The Poems of St. John of the Cross*, trans. Willis Barnstone (New York: New Directions, 1968 [or 1972]).

[2] André Breton, *L'Amour fou* (Paris: Gallimard, 1937).

turned into waiting for what can only treacherously fail the call, that this request is raised as a second call, for help against the melancholic distress that then seems to engulf the subject. Perhaps this subject also hurls himself into the analytic process when he finds himself condemned to deny the qualities of the woman or man who ravished him with a cruelty that startles him.

Passion and melancholy allow us to define the relation of the subject to the Other[3] and to otherness. If we admit that melancholy is the kernel about which passion is organized, if passionate indulgence is the paradoxical site that the melancholic haunts in an attempt at recovery, then we are entitled to ask ourselves where the Other, as the agent of unhappy *jouissance,* stands in this drama.

In each case, the person tormented by such affects abandons his position as subject. Subjected to the other, he is always the ravished one, never the ravisher. Or that, at any rate, is how he presents himself: as the toy, the *puppet,* the passive victim of his partner, whom he accuses of being the agent of his impassioned undoing.

In passion, the other (the object of the impassioned one's ardors) is expected to occupy the place, not of the good or bad object,[4] but of the scandalous one by whom the offense cometh, the one that flings the impassioned person into a drama in which he plays at shedding his signal traits—where he acts out "his defeat."[5] The melancholic designates the other as the cause of his passivity, agent of his distress. Like a believer who judges the coming of some scourge of God as inescapable, the melancholic declares himself guilty and with his own oaths summons an anonymous dispenser of justice to reveal to him the fault at the origin of his interminable self-accusations.

---

[3] The Other, that is, who internally represents all the wealth of signifiers (yet who can nevertheless be *imagined* as relay for the first Other, the mother).

[4] The cause has long been understood. It isn't a question of a good or bad object. There simply *is* the object, *good* and *bad* being terms that can simply be appended (alternately *good* or *bad,* depending . . .).

[5] Cf. Jacques Hassoun, *Les Passions intraitables* [Untreatable Passions] (Paris: Aubier, 1993).

The hypothesis I'll try to present through clinical fragments is as follows: The melancholic has had to cope with a mother who could not accompany him through weaning. If we consider that it is the mother who loses the breast, that the breast is never anything but provisionally appended to the mother; if we admit that it is the child who, in weaning, "gives up the breast," weaning would then constitute a ceding, a "transfer" in the legal sense. What happens, then, if one of the conditions of weaning has not been fulfilled—given that weaning is an experience shared by mother and child—if, for example, the mother, the first Other, is not in a position to give herself over to weaning?

Weaning presupposes that the mother is capable of realizing that it is she, in the nursing process, who loses the breast. "Her" weaning, then, is the precondition for her child's. In short, all she gets from the breast is its *jouissance;* and in prolonging that *jouissance,* she's barring the path to her child's rightful chance to "give up the breast."

From this point on, we can say that the child can give up only what has been constituted as lost by the Other. It is in this operation that the object is constituted. Which makes me wonder: If this "transfer," this ceding, is a surrender (there are breast-feedings and weanings that are surrenders for children), wouldn't the object be, at least in part, kept from loss?

Let me take this hypothesis further by recalling that if for Lacan the transitional object, "this little bit wrested from something," is as it were invested by *objet petit a*—the desire-causing object—it is still necessary for this object to have already been established as a "transferable" object, that is, one that can be given up: in fact, no object will be able to fill the function that Winnicott assigns to the transitional object unless *objet petit a* has itself already been established as a lost object. This significant precedence does not imply a preexisting or original object: at most it signifies the precedence in which (and by which) the subject is constituted.[6]

To clarify this set of propositions, I shall refer to the case of a child

---

[6] Let us emphasize: the subject is constituted in the movement that leads it to recognize, confront, and compare itself to the *object* in its function as *lost object.* Only then can the transitional object fulfill its function as placeholder.

confronted with the difficulty his mother had had in losing the breast, at a time when she faced a particularly painful bereavement.

This woman, an analysand to whom we shall give the first name Baheya, in utter distress in her work of mourning, came to request analysis: her father had just died in the Middle East, whereas she had been living in France for many years.

During one session, while finally starting to unburden herself of the premonitional dreams of catastrophe and destruction that haunt her nights and terrify her, she mentions her child—her youngest— her son, fourteen months younger than a little girl whose birth she'd welcomed. This little boy, then ten months old, had been developing normally so far; but since the death of his grandfather he could not, and would not, eat by himself. He never puts anything into his mouth, not a toy, not a morsel of food, nor any other object. He doesn't cry or holler, he's gradually even stopped prattling. This period in which nothing seems to be able to go into or come out of his mouth, is soon followed by a period of listlessness that alarms his mother. Little by little, then, in the course of our sessions, I hear of an apathy coming over this child that really starts to worry me.

Out of curiosity, I ask the analysand to describe the history of this child's feeding and that of her other children. She informs me that she nursed her oldest child, a girl, for fifteen months, and her second child, another daughter, born two years later, for ten months. Furthermore, it's during this nursing period that she becomes pregnant for a third time. But with the birth of her son, she is suddenly exposed to the violence of her mother-in-law—a European—who insists that she not nurse this son so long. He is to be weaned at the age of three months. Several weeks later, the analysand's father would die in her native country. She immediately leaves her family, but arrives too late for the burial. Thus, not only has this analysand not had the time to reach the end of her weaning, but this weaning has coincided with the death of her father, a man of letters, a poet straight out of the pages of a novel by Tawfik el Hakim.[7]

---

[7] Cf. Tawfik el-Hakim, *Journal d'un substitut de campagne*, coll[ection] "Terre humaine" (Paris: Plon, 1974).

Which raises the question we must ask ourselves: Isn't it necessary in weaning for the mother to accompany the child in her own mourning? Isn't there, in this common path (of weaning) the child and its mother both tread, an experience of shared mourning? For this to take place, hasn't the mother needed to have time—the psychic time—to understand that the breast given is that part of herself she has detached and offered to the child? Isn't this the price paid for eroticizing the oral sphere? Isn't it what is lost by the Other, insofar as it is recognized in this status, that allows for this zone to be eroticized for the child, that is to say, marked, hallmarked, stamped with the seal of the signifier *loss?* Isn't it when the Other is proved capable of losing that part of self that allows a nursling to bind partial drives to the death drive? The lost object of the "first Other, the mother, as it happens" (as Lacan designates her) could not be represented here as a first model of object formation. In the absence of a lost-object-of-the-Other's-(f)act, victim-of-the-lack-of-deprivation, the melancholic, in the classic sense of the term or its symptomatic equivalences (anorexia, bulimia, drug addiction), by degrading and harming his body (sometimes to the point of subjecting it to someone else's perversion) tries to revive a cut-off or loss that did not take place.

Henceforth, the melancholic is this unseparated object that has failed to be. As such, he's a piece of trash trying to form itself as the cause of (non-)desire, of impossible desire, for anyone else likely to take an interest in him.

But if in passion a set of fragments of desire-causing objects has molded and condensed itself around the other who, in being passionately loved, is "raised to the dignity of being," in melancholia we witness a defection of drive whereby no one could ever prove (un-)worthy enough to support a cause literally lost in advance. "You'd have to be pretty worthless to lower yourself to my level of unworthiness"—so, in effect, runs the only formula that can account for this degeneration.

Now, in the transference, such a position on the part of the analysand can entail major difficulties arising either out of an exaggerated idealization of the analyst or out of a disappointment; whichever direction the difficulties take, they constantly endanger treatment.

It's as though the melancholic were asking: "What could the analyst's desire possibly be, what can its function be that it should lend an ear to a word that endlessly shapes the various figures of worthlessness and depreciation?"

The analyst—at times seen as an Other arising out of a general ferocity, at other times as a worthless piece of trash whose fecklessness is commensurate with the analysand's loss of will—may fill the place of an emptiness in the mirror: not the comforting figure who attests that the separating operation has been carried out and that the mirror image has been assumed, but rather the figure of a dense, dark opacity, an enigmatic object that bears in it all the stigmas of passion, from first astonishment to final dejection.

It is obvious that the analyst is called upon to be shifted, or more precisely, to shift the destination site of the analysand's speech. This is the minimal, necessary condition for introducing into the *failing,* or *falling short of [faute de]* that afflicts the melancholic analysand, a possible area for play and dialecticization, in other words, of loss. For the melancholic is tormented not by a loss, but by the lack of possibility for naming and designating this loss.

"I can't stop eating; all these weeks, I've been living huddled, bent on one single purpose: to fill myself up."

"Maybe a certain lack of (the baby's) nourishment is being made up for here."

My intervention startles Jezabel. At the next session she says how comforting it had been to hear that: it made her feeding herself no longer seem something monstrous, but gave her permission to acknowledge that she'd been missing out on something; that that appetite wasn't a symptomatic bulimia but a *different* appetite: the one she had not known before.

This off-the-cuff construction will inaugurate a shift that manages to release Jezabel from a fluctuation that's put the analyst in a (specular) position of both constant dismissal and utter fierceness. Or such at least is the path that Jezabel has taken to bring into her analysis the riddle of a desire capable of finding its cause and object. In fact, object formation in the transference and especially in the treatment of melancholics allows the analysand—proceeding at times from a complaint that seems endless—to bring significance to a symptom, to underscore its metaphorical dimension, to inscribe it within what has failed to occur so that, by such a series of displacements, he can finally grasp the dimension of desire in it.

Because in melancholia *summoning up the object* as "lost" assumes that it is as not-lost (hence not summoned, "non-occurring"), that it manifests itself for the melancholic as a cause of the suffering and inability to mourn that has oppressed the subject.

In fact, if in passion, the object that is cause of desire seems to lose its function by becoming identical to the persona on which the impassioned person has set his heart and to whom he has subjected himself, in melancholia what signals and causes the defeat of drives is the very lack of a gap on the part of the object, which prevents the melancholic from investing or desiring anything. This impossibility baffles him by the deadly, redoubled weight of bereftness it imposes.

In this regard, Jezabel's history seems exemplary: After several months of hospitalization in a private clinic, Jezabel begins her analysis inauspiciously enough. Nearly fifty, she was married at age eighteen, mainly, she says, to escape being the only child of terrorizing parents. Through the years, she's forged a bond—an extremely rapacious one—with a very caring, tender husband. Then suddenly, after twenty-eight years of marriage, he ceases to "honor" her. She tries everything to win him back, but it's useless. Now Jezabel, persuaded her husband is simply a casualty of "the age barrier," falls back on her numerous offspring to whom she devotes herself with real intelligence. Also, she seriously nurtures her writing activity, quite successfully in fact. Years go by, then one day she decides to extract a confession from her husband: whereupon he admits that for five years he's felt no desire for women. He hasn't stopped loving her for some other woman, but—what's worse, in a sense—for no one, neither woman nor man. This withdrawal marked by a distaste for the female body casts Jezabel into a deep depression, during which she loses all self-esteem; when she does come out of her torpor, it's only to reel off an endless complaint. She knows, she says, whom she has lost, but not what she has lost, since that explanation can be given only by a man, and by one man only—the very one who's shirking his duty. This collapsing of *whom* she has lost into *what* she has lost sends her into a bottomless melancholic spiral [*mise en abyme*], a loss of self-esteem, the expression of something profoundly puzzling and distressing that definitely signals an inability to mourn. Henceforth, she no longer knows to whom she can turn to retrieve that part of herself that's gone astray. She knows and states very clearly that it isn't him she has lost but herself; in this whole turn of events, it is herself who has been swept away, adrift in a current that's annihilated her. Karl Abraham, incidentally, says something that applies point for point to Jezabel: that, in melancholy, "the shadow of the object has withdrawn from the ego," while in mourning, the shadow of the object "is cast over the ego to engulf it." And it's this withdrawal that is the cause here. "Something odd happened to him" is the very peculiar affect this analysand would have to describe (a common expression in melancholias prompted by a disaster of passion); we can expand upon this as follows:

- I've been wronged;
- something was taken from me;
- therefore I'm unworthy, and my history is one of a long, perpetual disgrace.

All in all, the melancholic fails where the paranoiac succeeds[8]: for whereas the latter manages successfully to create external persecutory objects, the melancholic founders in a universe of misfortune with no assignable cause.

---

8 This sentence echoes—by inversion—Freud's remark: "I have succeeded where the paranoiac fails," in Sigmund Freud to Sandor Ferenczi, October 6, 1910, *Correspondence*, trans. *Coq héron* (Paris: Calmann-Lévy, 1992), 231.

Jezabel will apply this querulousness to herself while vaguely demanding that the other grants her what, by definition, he cannot possibly give her, which over and over again will allow her to reinforce the feeling of decay and worthlessness that pervades her. She is deprived of the one object that can fill this abyss she carries about inside her, opening at every moment beneath her feet. This justifies the question that clinical practice poses to us: Is there any place for the other in the orgiastic *jouissance* typical of melancholics?

At the height of her distress, Jezabel seems to have fallen prey to a sexual drive directed toward what's lacking: a lack born from the unbinding of drives, in which the obscurity of a stated confession has merged with a demand addressed to a husband whom she, at an utter loss, relentlessly assails. Here death and life alike seem impossible, in this eruption over what is lacking.[9]

Love and hate—more than present—seem to be at the origin of a guilt that prompts Jezabel to say that she is "guiltier than everyone else combined," guiltier than her father, whose indifference and mildness have masked an extreme cruelty, guiltier than her mother was when she vanished once and for all from her marital home to assert "her right to orgasm": Jezabel launches into self-flagellation over her worthlessness and her desire to be filled by the man who's abdicated responsibility. Hers is a *demande* in both senses of the French word—an insistent demand and a question—since she knows that demand can receive no possible answer but one that tragically returns to the inert part of her companion's body, a part called upon only to satisfy self-withdrawal. The odd thing is that Jezabel seems poised at the juncture between mania and melancholia, the precise convergence point between hatred and self-depreciation.

---

[9] This "defeat of the drive that requires every living thing to cling to life" long surprised Freud . . . until he started writing *Beyond the Pleasure Principle*. Our hypothesis would be as follows: The paths of the drive are, tangentially, placed one by one in the service of passion, whereas in melancholy (which may ensue) the drives *erupt*. It is then that the melancholic seems in the immediate grip of the death drive, which appears to affect all paths of the drive.

To grasp this hypothesis, I urge the reader to go back to Dostoyevsky's *Notes from Underground,* a long monologue much like one a melancholic would deliver in the course of his gloomy ruminations in order to present himself to us as racked not by suffering, but by guilt without a cause:

> The main thing is that, however you look at it, it always turns out that you are chiefly to blame for everything, and what hurts most of all, innocently to blame, by the laws of nature, as it were. I am to blame because, first of all, I am cleverer than anybody else around me. . . . And, finally, I am to blame because even if I had had any generosity of spirit in me, it would only have been a greater torment to me to realize its complete uselessness. . . . Finally, even if I refused to show any generosity of spirit, but wanted to be revenged for the insult, I couldn't even take my revenge on anybody for anything, because I should probably find it impossible to make up my mind to take any steps, even if I could.[10]

Dostoyevsky credits this sentiment to a keen sensual pleasure derived from a particular humiliation that seems to go beyond laws both human and natural. To speak of the "impossible"[11] refers to a common fate. But the melancholic experiences this "impossible" at every moment. He brushes up against it constantly, nourishes himself upon it. At the depths of the abyss he plays, like some godhead, with that impossible aspect of utter ruination and decay he attempts to reach by horror and apathy. The melancholic, in the obscenity of the permanent complaint and the horror he doles out to all and sundry, is potentially a maniacal god, triumphant, deafening, devouring, and, if truth be told, prey to a passion we must recognize under all that apathy and ostensible indifference toward the world and toward others.

---

10 Fyodor Dostoyevsky, *Notes from Underground/The Double,* trans. Jessie Coulson (New York: Penguin Books, 1972), 19–20.

11 Lacan, in his *Quatre Concepts fondamentaux de la psychanalyse* [The Fundamental Concepts of Psychoanalysis] (Paris: Le Seuil, 1973, p. 55) writes that "at the origin of psychoanalytical experience the Real has been presented in the form of what about it is *unassimilable*—in the form of trauma, determining its entire outcome, and imposing on it a seemingly accidental origin." It is thus that in the

Roger Munier writes:

> Melancholia knows that the world is perishable and approaches it
> accordingly. Nothing out of the ordinary in that, it would seem. But
> knowing the world to be perishable and living in it with that knowl-
> edge is not such a frequent, or such a simple, thing. We know very
> well that the world is perishable, but not now, in the here and now.
> We know that it will pass away, but after, in an after as unlikely, after
> all, as our own death. We don't approach the rose in bloom, in all its
> beauty, as we do the rose that will fade, whose withered, livid petals
> will one day bestrew the ground. To know that the rose is perishable,
> not someday but now and evermore, is a different, poignant kind of
> knowledge. This is what melancholy bids us acknowledge, if we
> follow it to the bitter end. . . . Thus it thwarts Power in two ways. It
> holds it at a distance, recognizing it for what it is: Potency, yes, in all its
> vigor and beauty, yet threatened in its very workings, destined one
> day to negation. . . . Melancholia . . . leaves nothing outside its field.
> It tampers with the divine and the terrestrial alike, and, to my mind,
> in two ways. It tampers with it by engulfing it in its dark foreboding.

Lacanian representation of the Real, the Symbolic, and the Imaginary, the Real is that
which forms an obstacle to the pleasure principle. It is beyond the *automaton*, that is, the
return, the ins(is)tance of signs. It is that which eludes symbolization, it would even
represent that which in a first phase, at least, is manifested as something impossible to
symbolize. Thus, in clinical practice, we can say that certain historical experiences that
present themselves as the eruption of unprecedented, unexpected violence that induces
fright, can appear to remain outside of any symbolization. It is as such that these events
partake of the Real. In the categories of the impossible such as Lacan maps it, we should
mention here his aphorism, "there is no sexual relation" [il n'y a pas de rapport sexuel]
(cf. Jacques Lacan, "La Logique du fantasme," [seminar presentation, March 8, 1967
and April 1, 1967]; likewise, cf. "Radiophonie," *Scilicet* [Paris: Le Seuil, 1970], 65)
and *Le Séminaire, Livre XX, Encore* [Paris: Le Seuil, 1975], 131)—i.e., it is *impossible
to write something that creates a relation between a woman and a man.* It is remarkable, moreover, to note—not without humor—that this "impossibility to write" is not
some sort of wall or a barrier erected before the "sexual relation," for in this regard
Lacan will say: *"ça ne cesse pas de ne pas s'écrire"* [this doesn't stop not writing itself].
That is to suggest how much the sexual relation relates to an ever-renewed effort to
achieve "this rapport" which can neither manage to be achieved once and for all nor,
for that matter, to succumb to "there is not," as it seems to present itself in the melancholic's *jouissance.*

And it tampers with it, otherwise perhaps, for the sake of this fore-boding, if not by this very foreboding.[12]

If we are to credit these authors—and how should we not, since clinical practice, however little heed is paid to it, is with them on this, indeed, all the way to Cotard syndrome[13]—then we must admit that the feeling of omnipotence is inseparable from that endless lament the melancholic rehearses ad nauseam. It is a matter of recognizing it and getting the melancholic to do so too in the transference. This almightiness, like the one that envelops a child who cries and expresses an absolute need, would seem to be the reverse of the one lodged in the impassioned person at the stage of encounter, discovery, assumption of his image projected in the gaze of the other.

In the end, what allows us to declare Jezabel a melancholic, when we might have supposed we were dealing here with a reactional depressive episode, hinges on this fact: that for several years she has accepted as a matter of course that her husband should be deficient. His "distraction," which didn't affect her one bit, seemed to strike the melancholic core that had always been working away in her; she had gotten only what she deserved and her self-aversion found full satis-faction in her husband's desertion. Her self-reproaches, her self-depreciation came, even before they could be expressed, from "the 'for' and 'against' contained in the conflict that has led to the loss of the loved object."[14]

Henceforth, her "plaint" would make her a "plaintiff,"[15] to borrow Freud's argument in "Mourning and Melancholia":

---

[12] Roger Munier, *Mélancolie* (Paris: Le Nyctalope, 1987), 60–62.

[13] An extreme form of delirious melancholia, in which the inner organs, one by one, are subjected to fantastic transformations, extraordinary alterations, in short, to attacks the subject experiences as cosmic-scale phenomena. In "le Cotard," there is no room for change—which also means no room for death.

[14] Sigmund Freud, "Mourning and Melancholia," in *General Psychological Theory* (New York: Collier Books, 1963/1968), 169.

[15] I am particularly struck by this "complaint-lodging," or "presenting of grievances," on the part of melancholics. In 1975 I had presented a text in a lecture in the seminar of

Their complaints are really "plaints" in the legal sense of the word[16]; it is because everything derogatory that they say of themselves at bottom relates to someone else that they are not ashamed and do not hide their heads. Moreover, they are far from evincing toward those around them the attitude of humility and submission that alone would befit such worthless persons; on the contrary, they give a great deal of trouble, perpetually taking offense and behaving as if they had been treated with great injustice. All this is possible only because the reactions expressed in their behavior still proceed from an attitude of revolt, a mental constellation which by a certain process has become transformed into melancholic contrition.[17]

"Identifying the ego with the abandoned object" and facing a devastating de-eroticized sexuality, a wordless, loveless sexuality, without tenderness, mute—this would seem to be the secret of Jezabel's melancholia. Which explains her desire, for the first year of her marriage, to have been born to her husband, rather than to what has taken her back to a primal scene caught in the Real of an inert, obscene parental sexuality. Also, as soon as her husband turns away from her, not for some other woman, but for *no other* woman, she finds herself having to identify, to the point of outright duplication, with her mother's shabbily orgiastic fate. This is not hysterical identification—the object isn't being erotically invested, after all—but it is a panic-inducing one: the object has not been lost, but has, as it were, always been abandoned. This abandonment of the object leaves a certain amount of love floating and highly ambivalent, of a sort apt to trigger hatred and sadism, vindictiveness and petulance— a prospect that seems to illustrate perfectly this statement of Freud's:

Moustafa Safouan, entitled "Women's Complaints" [La Plainte des femmes] (published in *Fragments de langue maternelle*) in which I related—completely unaware, I thought [of Freud's precedent]—feminine complaint to this "complaint-lodging."

[16] Freud, "Mourning and Melancholia," 169–170. [The original sentence reads: *Ihre Klagen sind Anklagen* (which might also be rendered in English as "Their griefs are 'grievances.' " Trans.]

[17] Freud, "Mourning and Melancholia," 169–170.

The occasions giving rise to melancholia for the most part extend beyond the clear case of a loss by death, and include all those situations of being wounded, hurt, neglected, out of favor, or disappointed, which can import opposite feelings of love and hate into the relationship or reinforce an already existing ambivalence.[18]

Thus, behind the incessant complaints, the notions of being wronged and unworthy, we cannot fail to recognize the eruption of a desperately damaged narcissism.

This body-abyss in which every orifice seems to have been (an-)eroticized, to the point that the subject seems no longer to face anything but an orgiastic Real, attests that we are not dealing here with the primal object, but with that part of the Thing [*das Ding*] that escaped murder, i.e. the symbolizing process that allows giving the object its status of lost object. It isn't mourning that occurs here, but an interminable state of bottomless, limitless bereavement. In manic-depressive psychosis, Karl Abraham tells us, crime is periodically renewed: never concluded, it is kept in abeyance from the mourning process.

Jezabel's recognition, at this bend in her marital problems, that she has been born to this particular couple of parents necessarily awakened the horror that has always been lurking in her: the horror of a body eroticized not by maternal discourse, but by the traces of the Thing, by that obscene part of a nonsymbolized mother, obscene to the point of fascination. So it was with horror that this conviction burst upon her: all these years her husband had been by no means an external object of love, but a trace of the unnameable. At first, however, he had offered her a way of escaping her damaged childhood; he allowed her to live by denying she'd been born to this family, this lineage. Then her husband's collapse left her disarmed, naked, trapped in the demand, begging that he might once more be granted his first, forever fled omnipotence. Reduced now to mere trash, she'd been devalued, become an insubstantial remainder she deeply hated:

---

18 Freud, "Mourning and Melancholia," 172.

"[She's] Wounded," he would repeat, "strangely wounded, like incapacity . . . but he is sovereign, like incapacity, and in his sense of abandon, of letting-be. Omnipotent incapacity."[19]

This, perhaps, is the paradox of Jezabel's melancholy: only child of a literally absent mother and an infinitely grief-stricken father, she presents herself to us as bearing the mark of this maternal omnipotence which, she says, she has never been able to mourn. It's why she was so troubled about the mark of an incomplete weaning, one that kept her prisoner of a devastating orality, a passion in which the funereal seemed to surface out of jubilation and *jouissance*. Isn't this the testimony of Jezabel's passion when confronted with a transgression dictated by an imperious, deadly impulse to question a primal scene reduced to *mother-love* conceived as the "cause of all things"?

We can postulate in fact that passion is a compromise formation toward a silent melancholic core that may also be tinged with hysterical as well as phobic, or even at times perverse, symptoms. This hypothesis would account for those cases in which all the stakes of a passion seem to come down to the supposition that the father's family honor has been stained, a revelation which, in an existential crisis, causes a melancholic *mise en abyme*.

If, furthermore, we consider that love is founded on a signifier, a signifying articulation, whereas in passion a sign is the basis for the encounter, then we must draw various conclusions from this hypothesis. Henceforth, the being by which the subject will be alienated will embody, through this sign, an Other without phallic reference, as though situated beyond castration. This absence of reference proceeds from a disconnection of drives that combines boundlessness and immortality to the triumph of a desubjectivizing process.

In its mingling of a lover's fluster with filial panic, "if passion is," in Georges Bataille's terms, "the most moving reality . . . it is, at the

---

19 Munier, *Mélancolie*, 64.

same time, also the vilest . . . it is horrible, it is tragic, it is inadmissible, the more divine it is."[20]

Horrid and vile, passion may be said to be the exact opposite of melancholy. It affirms, it makes claims where the melancholic submits; it burns and consumes itself where the melancholic sadly stirs the cold ashes of his failures and his impossibilities.

Roxane was to encounter this extreme ferocity when the death of her lover, whom she had left some weeks earlier, revealed to her what her passion had been, through a long bout of melancholia that lasted nearly two years.

What happened was this: Roxane, in the course of an analysis that had thus far gone without any major hitches, suffered a catastrophe within a matter of a few hours: her friend Twist, about whom she'd spoken very seldom up to then, met with a brutal death. Up to that point, her talk had centered on her parents' divorce in the wake of her father's going bankrupt; she'd described herself as trapped in the "oversexed" nature of her mother and her subsequent lovers, whose seduction and onslaughts she had to endure, but trapped as well in a poverty she'd known for years.

Now, one day, her friend, with whom she had incidentally stopped living, was hospitalized: stricken with a severe nephritis, extremely cirrhotic, his body could no longer hold up. For several weeks she nurses him night and day. She leaves him only to go to work; one day, while she's out for several hours, he dies.

Roxane then sinks into massive depression. She is hospitalized for several weeks, no longer eats, no longer leaves her room, or even her bed. Four months later she resumes her analysis, reduced to the state of what the inmates of concentration camps called a *Musulmann[er]*: subjected to an inscrutable and absurd regimen, she is willing to die off. From now on she depends on the man who depended on her. At the boundary of the Real and the Imaginary there looms this

---

20 Georges Bataille, "Les formes composées de l'érotisme," Part 6 in *Oeuvres complètes*, vol. VIII, *Histoire de l'érotisme* (Paris: Gallimard, 1976).

place of identification that suspends her life in a state of minimal tension. She's identifying with a dead man who offers himself to her as a corpse, a destroyed body she can longer leave. Within herself she carries the man to whom she's now united in nonlife. No longer is he drugged, alcoholic, capricious. He's out-of-tension. She carries within herself this inert corpse who abolishes all tension, hunger, thirst, or lover's ardor. And the body Roxane herself carries about is transparent, her sorrowful face growing more beautiful by the day: she's in the state of grace of an autoerotic bliss, a zero-degree of tensions, a triumph of the pleasure principle so complete that it no longer suffers the least boost of energy, but rather seems to have opened to her—in her own lifetime—the gates of an eternal repose, an immense, unutterable, infinite happiness.

Yet this second treatment took a turn when, during one session, I remarked to her—to my own great surprise—that, when all was said and done, she was trying to *give body to the other of suffering.* It was a matter for her, then, not of forming the other out of her masochism, but rather of calling this unnamed other of suffering into being. For, if this death had shown her that there was a prior unmournable grief, this still puzzling transformation of a living person into an imperishable corpse had made it obvious that for her, the only other she could conceive of was one bereft of life.

Gradually, starting with this intervention that recognized that her suffering stemmed from an encounter with a death she could not possibly mourn, Roxane was able to begin to establish what could allow her to deduce from this Other—enigmatic, terrifying, imperious—an otherness able to introduce a tension even within the Real of her agonies. This tension was undoubtedly painful. But it allowed her to give voice to the various figures of unhappiness that had hitherto occupied her psychic space, to the point of locating it in that terrifying region where melancholia turns into masochistic autoeroticism.

Twist had been the pretext for this frantic search for a *double in nature,* a clone who, no sooner than imagined, would make a great oak spring out of the anorexic acorn she carried in her. Twist's cadaverization--within his very lifetime—had proved during this analysis to be that share of impossible mourning that had never yet managed to manifest itself in her. Twist's death and her keeping him inside herself had allowed signification of what had always been silently operating in her, throwing her back upon the impossibility to formulate this statement: Ambivalence of feelings exists, and murder, and the wish to murder.

Now, it strikes me that if the signifier murder has not been able to receive a first inscription—the sort of murder of that ancestor Freud relates to the Father of the Horde[21]—then the path to the work of mourning is barred, like that of the various figures of difference and that of ambivalence. To erect within, in the inmost core of being, in place of an Other a corpse at once oppressive and superego-like was the price Roxane had to pay. The melancholia afflicting her activated one of the figures of the unspoilable, unnameable corpse, which condenses and makes a metaphor of what, having not yet attained the status of signifier, lingers as trace.

Roxane, after going through a long period of melancholia, had first to be able to connect the deterioration of a father omnipotent, omnisexual yet expelled from his paternal function, to her own collapse, to be able in a next phase to pry herself loose from the corpse, in order this time to have the subjectivizing experience of a mourning that had not yet taken place.

Finally, if we consider that the basis of existence lies in the bonds that the subject has managed to establish with the Other, we must ask ourselves about the function of the links the melancholic forges with those closest to him.

Is there an Other for the melancholic? Nothing could be less

---

21 The father of Freud's myth is by no means "paternal." Committing incest, aiming to have it all (all the girls, all the women, all the sons, all the goods), he seems rather to be one of the figures of an all-powerful mother (before which Freud could only recoil). Likewise, the murder of the father would seem to be the softened avatar of the murder of the Thing (Sigmund Freud, "The Return of Totemism in Childhood," in *Totem and Taboo: Some Points of Agreement Between the Mental Lives of Savages and Neurotics*, trans. James Strachey [New York: W. W. Norton & Co., 1950]). Or so, at least, we can understand it today.

certain. What would this Other be? What would be its function, given that the melancholic is a child abandoned too early by a mother too absorbed in contemplating her own image? This mother, by the way, is not distracted. She is absent for her child and for the man who would occupy a position of father for that child. She is present only to herself. How, then, is one to introduce the Other into the treatment?

When Lacan said that human desire is the desire of the other, he let it be understood that the first object of desire is founded upon the desire to be recognized by the Other. Let us assume then that this Other refuses to recognize us, that at the moment, say, when the child turns to its mother to seek out in her gaze what will support the outlines of its mirror image with recognition, she turns away her head or offers the child an empty gaze. What can come of this but a meeting with the impossible? Desire will now be more or less suspended. At a crucial point—the founding point of recognition, i.e., the point that also permits identification—the place of the Other is mute.

The Other's muteness and blindness, its indifference to being addressed, cause a shattering in the subject that lands it this side of mourning. We can say of melancholics that something befell them, "fell their way," in the sense that their speech fell on deaf ears, was lost in limbo. Here the letter is no more lost than it is in suffering; it's questing after a receiver, so that that it finally can be written. One step further and the very notion of a letter fades: "I must do something, but what?" Then the dreary weight of "I've nothing to do, I'm good for nothing," increasingly sets in and invades the psychic landscape. This considerable distress results in that anxiety-less suffering that is the lot of the melancholic.

Let us try here to trace the genealogy of this assumption by referring to the distinction Lacan draws between demand, need, and desire: "Demand," he says, "tears itself loose from need,"[22] separates

---

[22] Jacques Lacan, "Subversion du sujet et dialectique du désir," *Écrits* (Paris: Le Seuil, 1966), 814.

itself from it. This rending conveys to us that the demand relates to a declaration of love, an address to the other, a *je ne sais quoi* that represents an appeal to satisfaction which the other can only partially confer.

Demand, then, is like the opening up by way of "the second nipple," "the second baby bottle," of a feeling of surprise and of nostalgia. Something of the need is satisfied, *almost nothing* separates this second partaking from the first, this *almost nothing* forms an edge. This edge can be said to follow the borders of the rending that separates and unites (as scar, as trace) the need and the demand. It is in this edge that desire is situated, set into play by drive-related activity. We see, then, how essential it is to separate drive, internal and historicizing, from instinct, external and subordinate purely to the categories of necessity and survival.

If we grant that "desire is sketched out in the edge where demand tears itself loose from need," we realize that this configuration of need-desire-demand defines the subject, or more precisely, represents it.

Such an arrangement seems to me to bring some clarity to Lacan's three propositions, and I think it's timely to recall here:

> "The object of desire is an object rescued from the waters of love."
> "I move forward in the world of objects only by the path of objections to my desire. The object is found by way of objections."
> "Desire is sketched out at the edge where demand tears itself loose from need: this edge being that which the demand . . . opens up in the form of the possible lack that need can bring to it, of not having universal satisfaction (which is called: anxiety)."[23]

We might also say that if the object as cause of desire is rescued from the waters of love ("mother-love"), this is surely because demand finds a limit set upon its claims.

From this point of view we can better understand objections to desire: where the drive fails its object, desire finds its spur and its

---

[23] Ibid.

launching site [literally: deployment space]. What could create an objection to desire? Love[24] which tends to coincide with the object to the point of removing the dimension of pleasure from dalliance.

Let's go back to a possibility I broached earlier. Assuming that the path of demand (expressed toward the Other) is barred, the child will then be faced not with objections but with the impossible. Here anxiety vanishes and the topological order of need/demand/desire collapses. An object remains, relegated to the status of a stopgap,[25] confronting the subject with a terrifying Other he must ward off.

Melancholics, then, are those for whom the Other's lack of recognition makes it impossible or risky to formulate a demand, those whose desire remains a riddle and who—meeting less with objections to their desire than with objections in the legal sense: blunt refusals, demurrals—see their relation to the object so impaired that they find themselves fixated in an endless state of grief, with no possible recourse to anxiety, that is, to what could give rise to an object.

The void the melancholic faces marks the place of the Thing which comes to fill in for the object. This is why Roxane, who had had to regress to the point of obeying mere need, could break out of her state of apathy only at that moment in the transference that gave voice to her tendency to give body to the other of suffering. We can say after the fact that this Other was none other than the representative of the object's absence. The rest of the analysand's history amply confirmed this for us.

The Other of suffering (to say the least, an odd formulation that suddenly occurred to this analyst while listening with horror to a particularly chill pronouncement) shows that Roxane had as Other only the representation of this object-absence: her demand, expressed for a definitely absent—foreclosed—receiver, left her prey to a terrifying, naked, desperate desire.

---

24 Or more precisely, passion.

25 And no longer the status of lost object.

To link the Other to suffering, to say her task was to give bodily solidity to the Other, meant that in this unacknowledged suffering there was an Other, summoned into being by her, as addressee of her (com)plaint: namely, the analyst. In these circumstances, the suffering turning into a signifier could, in a first phase, be recognized in its object status, whereupon other objects were then able to appear. This means that in the analysis of melancholics (as much as, but often more than, in other treatments) we work to establish the object, work toward a mourning that was never carried out, bearing in mind—as François Baudry notes—that "the new love that is the very formula for the (analytic) act" tends to establish an object that can allow the subject to mourn.[26]

This *mourning for:* Isn't it what we immediately encounter in every request for analysis? Can't one claim here that this demand always masks a secret passion, misconstrued and hanging on an unuttered word?

The fact that the transference can work on what sets a limit, as well as on the part of the Real that may take the forms of abjection, hate, and love (at the extreme), this is what allows for the subject's gradual introduction to the symbolic function, thus separating him from the avenging Commendatore's statue of the Don Juan myth that is the basis for passion, from inaugural kindling by thunderbolt to final decomposition. It is, then, by virtue of transference love[27] that the melancholic will be able to establish the object.

Only on this condition will solitude cease to beckon and access to the heterogeneous allow the melancholic to grasp that the [one] master that desire answers to is neither cruelty nor completeness, but lack.

---

26 Cf. François Baudry, *L'Intime* (Paris: Éditions de l'Éclat, 1988).

27 Sometimes after a detour through a passion for analysis or for the analyst, who will have—but is it any use to point this out?—to guard against yielding to it.

Chapter 3

"Je ne sais quoi . . ."

IF MELANCHOLICS, being at the mercy of a totalizing causality, are people hampered by what their mothers could not bear to lose, if they are refused the possibility of sharing with her the first object (the breast), they are also people who have experienced a terrifying intrusion they could not fend off. They are people who have been unable to find the *je ne sais quoi* that might have helped them erect some barrier against an invasion all the more troubling in being attributable to the woman who, at a crucial moment in their existence, was "not there for them."

Baheya's analytic history has allowed us to illustrate this hypothesis. Indeed, the work of mourning over a premature weaning allowed her, in retrograde fashion, to approach and then perform the mourning for her father. This twofold work was based on the fact that the violence she'd suffered at the hands of her mother-in-law helped her to acknowledge the intensified violence her own mother had directed toward her and which the death of her father had, to her enormous surprise, reactivated. All these years—since the revolt that had led her, thanks to her father's understanding but against her mother's wishes, to leave her native village for France—she had suppressed, then repressed, this fact: against the violence of mother, brothers, and cousins stood one lone rampart, and that one extremely frail, the *je ne sais quoi* that her father's saga represented.

Which raises a second question: Isn't the melancholic still in the throes of something that constituted a startling *je ne sais quoi* for the previous generation?

If we look back over Jezabel's case, this supposition is confirmed: in fact, her father, who had never been able to mourn for his own father—who was lost at sea in World War I—remained horrified by his own paternity, as he was of anything that might represent a manifestation of life. Jezabel could only accept this inconsistency which, at the moment of melancholic breakdown, could be translated as: "Before knowing *what* is missing, I know *that something I don't know of [je ne sais quoi]* is missing."

This *je ne sais quoi* designates what did not come into its proper place—in this case, access to the work of a primal mourning, representing that part of the other that is not absent, hence is immortal; yet absent too because it's unreadable and indefinable, this part is essential for the successive blackout [or disappearance] it brings on: "It is the only one worth the trouble of being spoken of and thus the only one of which one cannot speak."[1] Opaque, enigmatic, it represents itself indecipherably as what would de-eroticize not just a single area of the melancholic but the whole body.

For Eros must depart and the subject find himself deprived of whatever might serve to shore up the minimum of binding of drives necessary to do the work of mourning for someone close, or for some ideal, or some socially encoded entity, or simply for something uncertain, indeterminate that emerges from the subject's desire. Eros's fade-out will plunge the subject into an unfathomable sorrow and apathy. *Almost nothing* oppresses him, destroys him, fixates him, unleashing feelings of self-reproach and irritation, guilt, and worthlessness. *Almost nothing* divides him from a state of inconceivable happiness.

Almost nothing—of which the *je ne sais quoi* is the negative

---

[1] Vladimir Jankélévich, *Le Je-ne-sais-quoi et le Presque rien* [I-don't-know-what and Almost Nothing], vol. I, "La Manière et l'Occasion" [Manner and Occasion] (Paris: Le Seuil, 1980), 11.

definition—causes the subject's vacillation for a few days or for a few months, but sometimes also for a few moments, in a dismaying synchrony in which the different figures of loss and murder appear in alternation, plunging him into a melancholy that may occupy him—hold him under occupation, in a state of siege—for years.

This *almost nothing* isn't nothing. By the tenets of negative theology (from Meister Eckhart to Saint John of the Cross) it represents the surest definition of divinity.[2] The eruption of this *almost nothing* reveals its function: if the Other—in this case, the mother—truly incarnates that which can lose nothing, she, in her understanding of the *infans* [her hearing-out of the speechless child], fosters this almost nothing that becomes the first and last model that the subject will encounter over and over again along the whole path of life. The havoc this almost nothing can work is of two kinds.

The first might be illustrated by Roxane, who had the hardest time imaginable prying herself loose from a man she needed to leave and who, she said, counted for nothing in her life. No sooner was this *nothing* dead than it became the *almost nothing* of her existence. It took an intervention—an interpretation about the other of suffering—to lead her to the moment in which she could understand the horror that was depleting her of herself, so that she could then give a name to this nothing, that is, eroticize it. Having always been present, her melancholic state burst open in an aura of dread, incomprehension, and amazement provoked by this question: How can the disappearance of this *good-for-nothing* prompt such a disaster?

Which raises the question of object choice: How is it these women choose these particular men, when they are *nothing at all?* Were they not at the time absorbed in the disconsolate, nostalgic

---

2 Cf. Benito Feijo, *Le Je-ne-sais-quoi*, trans. Catherine Paoletti (Paris: Éditions de l'Éclat, 1989). The author remarks in this work that "Meister Eckhart maintains that God is a nothing [*ein Niht*] and God is something [*ein Iht*]. What is something is also nothing. . . . God is je-ne-sais-quoi [*neizwas*], which is very far above." This position is not so far removed from Jewish theology, be it the rationalism of Maimonides, or the mysticism of Isaac Luria.

complaint of an impossible original loss? Onto their sick, twisted companions, too often destined for sordid deaths, they carefully fashioned the reverse of the divine *almost nothing*, which might be called *inertia of insignificance*. It is incomprehensible to these women that they should lose these men precisely because they bear the mark of nonloss. It is a matter of a baffling disappearance that death reveals, one no prior signifier seems to have captured: "That couldn't happen to me . . . That man couldn't die . . . he could only linger on in the infinite decay that made me choose him in the first place."

It is then that this choice reveals itself for what it has been: staging and enacting of the worthlessness that had always inhabited Roxane, as she finally had stunningly confirmed for her.

To be sure, as Roger Munier reminds us, "melancholia knows the world to be perishable and approaches it through this dimension . . . here-and-now."[3] Now the choice of an object that bears decay in itself so actualizes the perishable that it can perish only with the melancholic. Melancholics anticipate the perishable, which as such cannot help but accompany them their whole lives. The death of this object plunges someone who always lived in the pathetic knowledge of the perishable into the indignity of living, hoping, desiring.

Thus, melancholics love "the rose already stripped of its petals and giving off the sickly sweet odor of the decayed"; for death, the desertion of a loved one or an ideal, cannot help but hasten them on toward this impossible question: How, being "secure" in this knowledge, could they live, desire, and love this decay? Aren't they already reduced to that even before that comes to them through the other? One question remains: Can the *almost nothing* allow us to understand the possible relation between femininity and melancholia?

If we hold to the Freudian postulate Lacan elaborated upon that the phallus—which cannot be specularized—takes the minus sign

---

3 Roger Munier, *Mélancolie*, 60.

$(-)$,[4] we may ask if, following the lead of negative theology, Freud and Lacan after him did not introduce a radical break in classical psychology by maintaining that the phallus cannot be represented or rendered positively, while still affirming its primacy and assigning all *jouissance* to the phallic, with one major difference: that women aren't entirely caught in phallic *jouissance*. A part of them partakes of an Other *jouissance* they share with the mystics.[5] This, then, is our hypothesis: Melancholics, when they register a de-eroticization toward the enigmatic thing defined as a *je ne sais quoi*, take imaginary castration literally as a truth of their decayed being, to the point of reuniting with the Other *jouissance*. This position would make melancholics mystics who forbid themselves to seek in any divinity a limit to their decline and drift. In this regard melancholics, in the desperate search for a good-for-nothing, a double in kind to further reveal to them their own wretched state, will continually refer to the phallus, taking seriously only the minus sign they remain in thrall to. At this point, this *almost nothing* will push melancholics to distance themselves from anything that might represent a cause of their desire, sinking into an indifferentiation that manages to suspend all desire. The turning in upon oneself, the primal narcissization [*sic*], the tendency to take the Ego for an object, endless complaints are corollary to this, until melancholics finally destroy the one object they can attain: the Ego.[6]

This hypothesis can help us to account for the occurrence of melancholics' suicides just when the symptoms seem to show signs of improvement. Coming up against anxiety, expelled from a death

---

[4] The phallus is viewed as the term that designates what, by not figuring into the specular image, founds it. It appears then, to use Lacan's own terms (in the seminar on "Transference"), as an island, the blank that on maps signifies the *terrae incognitae*. He adds that this "blank" is needed for the symbolic dimension of the Imaginary [register] to function. At this point, the only writing necessary for the phallus is the index of the minus sign $(-)$ (one of the ways to distinguish it from "what the man is afflicted with, the penis").

[5] Jacques Lacan, *Le Séminaire, Livre XX, Encore* (Paris: Le Seuil, 1975).

[6] Sigmund Freud, "Mourning and Melancholia," 169. He writes that melancholy is a purely narcissistic disorder of the Ego.

that seemed already to have come, they attempt to attack the existence of the last object they have available to them: their own body reduced to the status of a mirror image—the extreme, paradoxical point of rebinding of drives that appears unimpaired. The return to life in the high anxiety of rapture prompts a brutal disconnecting, an absolute state of panic. It is then that the object-Ego is assailed with full force by the death that annihilates it. A final success, a final attempt—dramatically—to summon some object in the wasteland that is theirs. Melancholics annihilate themselves where the *je ne sais quoi* has almost nothing left to attack.

So it was for Bernadette, who started her analysis after a suicide attempt. I'll cite only a few events from her history, among them this episode, which occurred at the time of the exodus in which she was abandoned by her parents in a wagon in the midst of a potato field, under bombardments. Later, she was placed in a boarding school where she received visits from her parents only twice a year. After moving to Paris, she gradually broke all ties with her family and learned of the death of her father only two years after the fact. Later, having become a mother herself, she was abandoned with her child, whose object she would become. She is now the victim of this daughter who, at the age of sixteen, beats her black and blue at the least pretext.

It's in the wake of one of these particularly trying clashes that she attempts suicide. Her treatment (which, for several semesters, was conducted face-to-face) took a spectacular turn the day she told me her dream of a weeping child. After, she was able to offer a construction that allowed her to say that if the child she had once been had been able to cry, it was because she perhaps had had at least an object to lose. It was then, in the moment its loss was revealed, that the object was established in the treatment: "I don't know what I lost, but I know that I did miss something, I've devoted all these years to my daughter to keep her imprisoned in that part of my self I've wanted her to merge into." Deprived of loss, unable to give it up— to cede it—abandoned, in a state of "lack of lack," such had been Bernadette's fate, which had brought her to the threshold of destruction and death.

This treatment managed to summon up the *je ne sais quoi,* and extricate Bernadette from "the absolute absence, so absolute that it is not even absence in the sense of deferred or lost presence;"[7] it allowed her to reach the *almost nothing* of nostalgia; then, gradually, to give up the weeping of an inconsolable child, ready at last to let herself be comforted.

---

[7] Roger Munier, *Mélancolie,* 29.

Chapter 4

"That man means nothing to me"

Passion has bored me for some time now, and I find a fuller truth in melancholy.

Letter from Chantal Steinberg
to the author

THE ABSENCE OF THE LOST OBJECT, the impossibility of mourning it, in short, the missing inscription of the signifier *mourning* that, however enigmatic it's become, still continues to beckon—these are synonyms of the disorder melancholia, an ailment that fills the subject with the image of a wondrous yet lugubrious object: the breast mother hasn't lost. Which leaves the question: What makes the mother "unable to lose the breast"?

Different hypotheses can be raised: For whom is mother saving this unlost thing—the breast? Is the melancholic the child of a couple too much in love? Is this child trapped in the "oversexed" scenario of his parents? Or is he not the offspring of a mother who assigns that child a place that allows it to sexualize "Mom" not in the interest of another, but at that of her own shaky narcissism?

Under such conditions, the melancholic is the child of a mother who never stops proclaiming: "That man, your father, means nothing to *me,*" a position altogether different from that of the mother who says: "That man, your father, means nothing to *you.*"

The difference is considerable. In the second case, the father, turned out from his paternal function, comes back as husband to this wife, the all-powerful mother of the psychotic, the woman who collects objects, who takes all and gives nothing. A veritable cemetery of the causes of desire, she literally aspires [breathes, that is] to people her inner world with what seems her due [her "revenue"].

As for the figure in the first case, the father can certainly exist in relation to the child, but this existence is accidental: this unloved man, this *je ne sais quoi* has failed utterly to move this woman, or in any case, to mark her.

The apparent impossibility to conceive in any way at all of this primal scene,[1] overwhelms the subject with bewilderment and apathy.

Who else before me has written that no one else before you was alive and no one was dying and no one was in me.[2]

Melancholics, in other words, come smack up against a radical absence, a withdrawal from time, a necrosis that attacks the body, from which life has withdrawn before it even was inscribed there. To pretend to live, a simulacrum facing a mere semblance of life, is the wearying task that rivets them to their inability to desire: what has been given them has immediately eluded them from the moment they entered existence.

In this necrosis, what belongs to You
and what is my lot, in this necrosis?
I wouldn't tolerate You without knowing,
You or I
or anyone else who slumbers in my name,
You who have mistaken me for someone else,

---

[1] This scene (the core of the fantasy) makes the subject the direct witness to his own conception.

[2] Thomas Bernhard, *Je te salue Virgile*, trans. K. Han and H. Holl (Paris: Gallimard, 1988), 24.

who has woken me up instead of someone else,
You who have shut me out of their vanity,
You who have conceived me, You my one and only poetry.[3]

These could well be the words of the melancholic. He occupies the place of another who could not accomplish what it is Eros's capacity to create: detachment.

What actually allows a mother to "lose the breast" is represented by a loss, the distant echo of her interplay with a man, not necessarily the biological father, of course, but the man who has represented and exercised the paternal function for this particular child. The corollary of the difficulty of getting the child to recognize his father as third party—as a man capable of arousing this woman, the mother—prevents her from losing the breast, losing what could allow the child to establish an object.

Melancholia is therefore always a question raised about feminine *jouissance:* not phallic *jouissance,* nor what has been labeled *jouissance of the mother*[4] (which would refer to psychosis), but rather a *jouissance* centered upon the seemingly untransferable object [unable to be given up]. To enjoy, indeed to "get off on" [*jouir*] this object in place and on behalf of "a man who's nothing to me" leaves the child out in the cold, the cold of melancholia.

How, in fact, can the child constitute the object as a lost object, if the first Other—his mother—has not been able to transmit to it an experience of loss? How can this mother set up the right psychic space for this operation, if this child is enmeshed in a linguistic sequence that continally proclaims of its father: "That man means nothing to me"?

This woman's object of lack finds no instrument of desire. The object of her lack runs up against insignificance. It is this that the melancholic will inherit.

---

[3] Ibid., 24.

[4] A reference to Lacan's double aphorism: "The mother's *jouir* is forbidden" and "To *jouir* over the mother is forbidden." [The mother is forbidden to get off, have sexual bliss, and it is forbidden to get off on the mother. Trans.]

To clarify: Love can arise only from the perspective of a word that demands a true hearing. In passion, there is only an endless, insatiable wait. Melancholics, of course, have given up waiting for anything. They despair of waiting and cannot utter the least demand. Love, Lacan tells us, is "giving what one does not have." Now, melancholics have been confronted with the impossibility of love, with the impossibility that the Other can be situated in loss, with the impossibility—in a word—of a gift, an impossibility that places their very being on the side of nothing. In other words, the child responds to the statement "He means nothing to me," which his mother's acted out, with an "I am nothing"; term for term (from the *he* to the *I*) this corresponds to the stations of a failed eroticization on the part of the first Other represented by the mother.

The work of mourning sets in motion a real object loss that can, piece by piece, sign by sign, ideal by ideal, truly validate that which sustains narcissism. Contrary to this, the melancholic has suffered such a deep narcissistic wound, such an absence of first eroticization, such a lack of love, that the mirror image—that which forms the basis for the ego and the ideals attached to it (Ego Ideal and Ideal Ego)—is incapable of supporting any mourning process whatsoever.[5]

Indeed, if the ideal is founded upon a loss and this loss has not been formed as a primary experience, then the ideals get tossed back into the limbo of the unnameable and the uninscribable.

Let us recall here that melancholics are bereaved people no mourning can possibly penetrate, since their state of decline cannot be measured by the standard of a radically absent ideal. They can only accuse themselves of a crime more heinous, more terrible than all crimes ever perpetrated or to be perpetrated: the crime against an absent object. They have killed no one in effigy. They have killed the absent one, male or female, have driven the object to suicide, the only object that counts, that's worth anything: the one that causes their desire.

---

5 Jacques Lacan, "Transference" seminar (June 7–28, 1961), from unpublished transcript.

What does it mean if that object was an *objet a,* an object of desire, except that that object is always masked behind its attributes. The business begins only with melancholia. In it, the object is much less palpable for being certainly present and unleashing catastrophic effects, for threatening the fundamental *Trieb*[6] that attaches you to life.

Freud registers a certain disappointment he cannot define. What will we see there, for such an obscure object? The object the subject attacks has none of the traits of an invisible object, [but] we can find some such traits from his own characteristics: I am nothing.

It is not the mirror image that is aimed at. It is in the realm of self-accusations, in the realm of the symbolic, having included: he is ruined.

Doesn't this tell you something? This convergence point is one neither of mourning nor of depression over the loss of an object, but of a certain type of *remorse* triggered by the *suicide* of the object.[7]

How are we to construe this "suicided object after it has entered the field of desire," except as the thing that reveals the scandal of what has not occurred in the first place and thus has failed to start a series?

The melancholic's object has killed itself only to the extent that through it the scandal of an absence has been revealed to the subject. Nor is it just any object: it has greater value than some other object, because, although it's the first, it does not give place to a series. As such, it is unique and terrifying. It calls into question the safety that a boundary offers, since it is able to reveal an incestuous limitlessness.

> This limit, which always calls into question *the safety of the limit,* is what is involved in the point of the fantasy we must know how to deal with. . . .
>
> What is at stake in this field of being that love cannot circumscribe is something about which the analyst can think only that *no object can replace it.*

---

[6] [*Trieb:* drive; French: *pulsion.* Trans.]

[7] Lacan, "Transference" seminar (June 7–28, 1961), from unpublished transcript.

We are led to wavering over the limits where this question "Who are you?" is posed with any object that once enters the field of our desire. There is to be no object more valuable than any other.[8]

Remorse, then, does not follow the suicide of the object: it precedes it. Faced with a possible desire, the object will be "suicided" through remorse. It is then that the remorse and self-accusations that proclaim the disgracefulness of having encountered this object take shape.

If murderers, in their guilt, kill to have their guilt acknowledged (and perhaps at a later stage to feel remorse for it), melancholics, consumed by remorse and pathetic nostalgia (for haven't they served as a prop for revealing a devastating "he means nothing to me"?), will try their utmost to destroy and be destroyed. Melancholics are products of a destruction whose agent they would be. They are guilty of the worst misdeeds and say so, only no one's willing to listen. They cry out for the Law in all its severity to free them at last from this overwhelming, crippling remorse, so that finally their guiltiness will make some sense. But, horribly enough, this murder has never been recognized by the Other, so the whole thing has to start over again and again!

Scions of a de-eroticization, melancholics are people for whom one object, when it presents itself, becomes so dangerous it makes them waver between *jouissance* and dejection in the quest for a murder they have not carried out, though they bear all the blame for it. This object is the inalienable, ever-inaccessible part of the Other.

In this regard, we can say that the melancholic is rather like a saint who moves entirely between having and destitution. Like those anchorites who haunted the deserts of Egypt and Judea in the early days of Christianity, living in total apathy in the name of an absolute love for an enigmatic and remote, sublime and almighty divinity, offering the annihilation of their will to live and their physical decay to the one whose ignoble crucifixion they worship—and who is to

---

8 Lacan, "Transference" seminar (June 7–28, 1961), from unpublished transcript.

be worshipped only by the grace of his ignominious death—the melancholic lives in the immobility of a paradoxical having, that of a love emptied of all desire.

Dürer has given us a glimpse into this experience of stasis, bestowing on our fascinated gaze the immobility of time and the elements.

All images are silent, or were at least before film and television. But few, it seems to me, are more silent than Dürer's *Melancholia*. The bell's clapper is perfectly vertical. Not the slightest breeze is stirring. The sea is slack. The two pans of the scale are perfectly balanced. The dog has gone its rounds. The sand of the hourglass has run half its course: time is halted; or rather, it can no longer be measured, for we know that although it is passing objectively, in the image, subjectively, all is motionless and silent.[9]

This immobility, this silence, accounts for a surfeit represented by the object which, ravished by the other, could not constitute itself as lost object, burdens and cloys the melancholic to the point of suffocation.

In fact it was quite necessary for there to be an object, since the melancholic is alive. But this object has been supplied, not given: it is inert. For that child the mother withdraws into herself; the terrible figure of an underworld deity, she continually proclaims: "I won't say no!" all the while maintaining the inertia of a delivery woman for whom the recipient and the object sent are sheer matters of indifference. So the melancholic has no other choice but to try to carry out the murder of the object.

So, at least, is how I understand the nature of melancholy cruelty: melancholics are no less cruel to those in their inner circle than to themselves. And they are this way, in short, since in order to rouse or summon into being the desire-causing object, they are constantly subject to the need to murder what strikes at the very heart of their subjectivity—to slowly murder those they love.

---

9 Maxime Préaud, *Mélancolies*, Format/Art coll. (Paris: Éditions Herscher, 1982), 6.

Remorse is a product of this murder, this always bungled, always unfinished suicide. Faced with the neverending task of a constantly recommenced suicide, melancholics sink into listless bafflement. They never doubt that the crime has already taken place and, at every instant, is perpetrated anew. Melancholics are gravediggers of their own history, stunned archaeologists exhuming no end of blanched bones, witnesses of an unimaginable, petrified life.[10] They range over Pompeiis where the bodies overtaken by lava are nonetheless deprived of any feature that could identify them.

Being mere decay himself, the melancholic lives in the interstice of constant decomposition. Like Saint Simeon the Stylite as Buñuel depicted him,[11] he stands firm amid the stench and decay. Perpetual prey to life's temptations, to the seduction of a female demon bursting with femininity yet who turns out to be a decrepit old woman with dried up teats and gray, sagging skin, he contemplates, through this repulsive being, his own glorious decline.

To this figure we might apply the words of Heraclitus: "Before every expression, man, stupidly inert, is wont to flare up with passion."[12] Living off only these passions that keep damaging them all the more deeply, melancholics show how to "give body to the Other of suffering," one way among others to rouse remorse for existing, for keeping up one's survival indefinitely. One step more and we enter that dark area at the borders of melancholy and masochism where we encounter those who seem doomed to take their own bodies as the object of their desire in order to survive.

To recognize oneself as an object of one's own desire is always masochistic.[13]

---

10 "Object of melancholia, Death itself is melancholic. The skeletons miss the flesh that enveloped them, the ghosts wander the earth anguished and sad, under the calm gaze of those who know enough to see them." Préaud, *Mélancholies*, 86.

11 In his film *Simon of the Desert* (1965).

12 Giorgio Colli, *La Sagesse grecque*, vol. III, *Héraclite* (Paris: Éditions de l'Éclat, 1992), 103.

13 Jacques Lacan, "Anxiety" seminar (January 9, 1963).

At the end of the 1970s Dominique had asked to enter analysis. At the time he was living in a small provincial capital in a country bordering France but, he told me, he couldn't see any of the analysts in his own city. He had been either their lover or their wives', or in any event knew them too well. So, for the first three years of his analysis, he would undertake long night journeys that would bring him to my office dirty, sweaty, and unshaven.

Dominique always wears a look of astonishment. His voice, his talk, his manner are those of someone perplexed, who doesn't understand what is happening to him or has happened to him. The child of a couple that quickly divorced, he alternated living between his mother and his grandmother up until the age of eighteen. His father, a small country squire, lives in retirement on his property. He remarried a very young woman who "prevents Dominique from meeting his father."

About his family history and his childhood he will say nothing. He talks of other things: wearily describes his life from week to week. He's worked in a circus as a tightrope walker and contortionist, has taken "semi-hard" drugs, has played—and for the first two years of his analysis continues to play—the role of clown and underdog in a gang of "leather men" he hangs out with. Among the little humiliations he endures, one of the most harmless is this: out one evening combing the countryside with his friends, he suddenly finds himself stripped of his shoes and (some of) his clothes and forced to walk fifteen kilometers to reach—quite naked—the patrician city he lives in.

As for his sex life, it consumes him: "He has to screw and screw" and when "it's over" he asks his partner to throttle him so that he can "get one more hard-on." Sometimes when he's alone, he hangs himself, masturbates wildly, sticks pins into his nipples and testicles to get an erection before sodomizing himself. He's well aware that "that's something not quite right." He's reached a point where his behavior scares him, but he doesn't really know why he should forbid himself these practices (he's very much surprised, by the way, that I show any disapproval toward these excesses). First and foremost his questioning concerns his emotional muddle, his alcoholism, his feeling of being a puppet, unable to change anything in his life no matter how he tries.

After some years, a certain change occurs. He resumes his university studies, marries, leaves his native city in order to settle in the Paris area, becomes the father of a little boy and under quite trying conditions a successful teacher in schools where few teachers last more than a year. He sets up a teaching program for children of non-French-speaking immigrants, makes contact again with his father, and slowly but surely gains prominence within his school district. Permanent conflicts remain, however, with his wife ("a gypsy who yells all the time"), and at moments the sexual frenzy of earlier days violently returns, only laced now with an edge of anxiety. Finally, it's hard for him to adapt to the rules of society: it's impossible for him to file his taxes on time, to pay his rent; he neglects filling out the various administrative documents that are part of any normal citizen's life.

So, little by little after the sexual masochism Dominique seemed trapped in has gradually been dispelled, there appear (like some text written on a magic slate) the real stakes of the game: what Freud calls a "moral masochism," in which passion always risks foundering.

Does this process reveal, as Freud posits, a relation to blame and guilt, so that the subject never stops wanting to punish himself? Or is it a matter, rather, of defying the Law and its upholder, the father? And within such a problematic situation, isn't this father a despot capable only of issuing harsh, sadistic dictates?

What the perverse position maintains as a challenge is a radical doubt of the legitimacy of the position of the upholder of law, not only of the particular position of one who, to him, represents the Law (or claims to represent it), but beyond that of anyone who claims to speak in its name. The masochistic response—and we know what an important place it occupies in the perverse structure—draws its meaning here from its irreducibility to a manifestation of guilt that would imply that the Subject has appropriated the Law that condemns him. Masochism is first of all a denunciation of the sadism of the other. . . . It is true that one can, after all, arm oneself with the Tables of the Law the way others wield the whip, yet there is no more intervention possible from the ethical order from the moment its judgments can find their sanction only in acts that result in the pleasure felt by the accuser as well as by the guilty party. Note, however, . . . that at the very moment the one who judges also sees the legitimacy of his intervention radically contested, and by the same token sees advanced a thesis that . . . is very close to the psychoanlytic theory on the conjunction of the father's desire with his function as agent of castration, as a representative of . . . the law. . . . The attention he brings to questioning the father's desire, to locating its fundamental place, grants him, in this ordeal, a special flair for recognizing essentials and knowing how to make use of the safest mechanisms.[14]

The safest mechanisms? Isn't this what the masochist is always paradoxically staging—a relation to desire that excludes any inhibition?[15] Isn't it because he sets up his desire as Law that the masochist finds himself fastened into the position of permanent loser? And is it in the perfect coincidence of desire with the Law that the masochist falls subject to a fierce superego that locks him into an ethic of failure taken to its logical end, but whose terms he seems unable to negotiate? The masochist is—like the sadist—one who, subservient to an unmoored desire for the Law, never yields to that which hurtles him toward these tragic impulses. The third is summoned as a witness, but in the altogether peculiar position of illegitimacy. Any intervention, any criticism, any remark, any interpretation intended to introduce any disjunction in the linearity of the masochist's discourse lies beyond his earshot, and can merely reinforce the law to which the pervert, and in particular the masochist, is subject: which only hastens their submitting to permanent self-punishment. And that's where the paradox lies: though blameless, the maso-

---

14 Jean Clavreul, "Le pervers et la loi du désir," in *L'Inconscient, Revue de psychanalyse* 2 (April/June 1967), reprinted in Jean Clavreul, *Le Désir et la Loi. Approches psychanalytiques*, L'Espace analytique coll. (Paris: Denoël, 1987), 202–203.

15 Ibid.

chist punishes himself without so much as broaching the notion of a sin or wrong or fault. If the signifier for wrongdoing is introduced into his talk, it represents nothing but a set of images that allows him to stage his perverse fantasies. The wrong he accuses himself of in order to be punished is more a matter of euphemism designed to maintain the real stakes he tries dramatically to set: to appeal more to the eye of the other than than to his ear. So we must regard masochism as an exhibition: it's a mistake to regard it as an inhibition. This exhibition consists of a paradoxical binding of drives: the death drive seems constantly active, shutting out the other in his subjectivity and taking one's own body as an object. Here the subject subjected to the law of Desire offers up his body and his fate to this eroticization of the death drive.

Now if we follow Freud in his statement that fate is the last figure—dread and inconceivable—of what the *infans* must deal with—parents—then we can consider that what is played upon as inconceivable for the masochist is precisely the parental couple he's come from. Won't being the child of these two people wreck the scenario of his desire, caught in the onesidedness of lack, in the supposed knowledge of the desire of the other, in the knowledge of his denial?

The masochist knows that he errs in this ultimate staging of a nonrelation with these parents, yet nothing of the consequences of this knowledge has been inscribed in his unconscious. In place of this absence of inscription there is only disavowal, the "I don't believe my eyes" whose ascesis he will uphold to the limits of his suffering.

The fact that confronting this secret, and its disavowal, can occasionally land the masochist in some pretty shady episode, still doesn't allow us to assume he's confronted a foreclosure of the Names-of-the-Father. What is at play here is ultimately an impossibility to recognize and identify the removed part of the first Other, the part that allows the subject to form a basis for his desire. It is this impossibility that comes out of an assumed disavowal toward the phallus and the Law insofar as they are upheld by the paternal function.

Indeed, if we can say that "the first renunciation of instinctual gratification is enforced by external powers, and it is this that creates morality, which expresses itself in conscience and exacts a further renunciation of instinct [i.e.: drive],"[16] then we can state affirmatively that the aforementioned external forces represented by the parental figures are, in masochism, the object of a disavowal requiring their object to submit to the fantasy "a child is being killed,"[17] which he will apparently be unable to give up for the rest of his life.

From this point on, what we are witnessing is the sexualization of the death drive and morality, whereby the outer world becomes the stage on which is enacted ad infinitum the punishment best able to provide the masochist proof of his own existence, in offering up his body to violence. This body-object, cause of the desire of the death drive, will attempt, through the suffering the Other demands, to encounter an elusive reality,[18] whereas closing down this path of access to the Other—and the suffering that accompanies it—becomes the law of the subject, his only Law. The superego *jouissance* that is at issue for the masochist is then taken over by a tension in drives that might not have found its limit in the aforementioned reality, in the outer world. Whence the frenzied encounter with suffering, and the need to encounter an other, if only in offering oneself to that other as an object; whence the point of contact and disjunction we discern now between melancholia and masochism.

In the first instance, the object, which was not established at the

---

16 Sigmund Freud, "The Economic Problem of Masochism," in *General Psychological Theory*, 190–201.

17 Jacques Hassoun, *Fragment de langue maternelle* (Paris: Éditions Payot, 1979), 64.

18 Let us recall that for Freud the reality principle is "a delay in the releasing of excitation and a temporary authorization of the tension of unpleasure." We can state, then, that the masochist is unable to submit to the reality principle, on the one hand, but that, on the other hand, this allowance to unpleasure returns him to the *jouissance* whose object his body has become. It is as such that this body of his, object of his desire, links up with reality. When all is said and done, for the masochist, it is the Real that takes over from reality. Cf. Sigmund Freud, "Two Formulations Regarding the Two Principles in Mental Functioning," in *General Psychological Theory*, 21–28.

time of primary narcissism, prevents a primal mourning—the model for future mourning—but by the same token it brings all-too-great a risk to a knowledge of loss and the lack-of-being; whereas in masochism, the avatars of the desire-causing object serve to support the sexualization of the death drive. This sexualization takes the body as an object, one means among others of placing oneself under the rod of a Law that attempts to know nothing of the lack in the Other (as founder of desire) in favor of a suture that the masochist, by the repeated wounds he has inflicted on his body, tries to preserve. The following formula addresses this masochist problem: to wound oneself, to bruise oneself, as long as the lack in the Other is not made possible much less, thinkable; to abase oneself in order to create a semblance of the Other even at the expense of a destroyed body.

It comes as no surprise that certain cases of substance abuse [toxicomania] or bulimia/anorexia border on melancholia and masochism, given the passion that sustains these addictions and the fact that passivity as a mode of relating to the other conjoins these different disorders, up to and including their relation to the anxious wait that would seem to be their common denominator.

Chapter 5

Where Passion and Anxiety Meet: The Wait

The object of desire appears as an object rescued from the waters of love.

JACQUES LACAN,
Seminar on "Transference"

CLINICAL PRACTICE teaches us that at the height of distress, melancholics are free of anxiety. Anxiety shows up only in those moments of remission that often delight those closest to the melancholics (worn out as they are by the long ordeal the patients have just gone through), to say nothing of fledgling psychiatrists and self-satisfied psychoanalysts.

The moment in which melancholics seem to pull themselves out of a long, murky nightmare is most often accompanied by what we would do well to call reunions with the object. The forms these take are quite peculiar: the appearance of this object does not rekindle desire or undo a gloomy, listless state of suspension; if anything, it should alert us [to possible risk]. The return to life leads subjects to recognize that they face (though they don't know since when) an enigmatic internal danger.

At the center of this turmoil, portending an as yet unrecognized anxiety, Freud places waiting and the indefiniteness of the awaited object. It is a matter, he tells us, of reacting to an internal, enigmatic danger. "I don't know what's going to happen to me, but this very ignorance means more than a knowledge, a certainty: it's certainly going to be dreadful." Or else: "Something is going to happen to me, but all I know is that the undecidable nature of this fatality means something dreadful's in store." These, more or less, are the formulas that account for the anxiety, though just uttering them entails a possibility of finding words for what can occur only in ignorance and confusion.

Be that as it may, this anxiety stages an event where nothing presents itself. In normal time we don't wait for an event. Something either happens or it doesn't. And what's likely to happen needn't be taken as the harbinger of a catastrophe or an endangerment of subjectivity. What, then, are the conditions for emergent anxiety? How can anxiety be inherent in a subjective situation?

Lacan, in his seminar of June 26, 1963,[1] says that anxiety, if it is without a cause, is not without an object. To understand this statement we must ask ourselves about the object of anxiety as it arises in passion and in melancholia and recall first of all that passion is the most spectacular mode of expression for a melancholic structure. Passion and melancholia on the one hand, melancholia and mania on the other, seem to set up a relation to the object of which melancholia is the key in that, being a symptom, it reveals—as I've shown—what is at stake in a child's relation to a mother who has been subjectively unable to help it through a first mourning process that grounds its subjectivity. This raises the following hypothesis: If anxiety arises in regard to a lack of object, it is presenting itself in place of the lack of the "transferable" thing itself.

Thus, the function of the child's crying (a cry that one refers to as anxious), which no object seems able to calm, requires a twofold plan:

- externally, it will search for the other, will try to reach it, simultaneously creating a potential space that could serve as a rift, or opening, in an overly close relationship;

---

[1] Jacques Lacan, "L'Angoisse" seminar (June 26, 1963).

- internally, it makes a hole in the overfullness, the lack of lack, which is at the origin of a first impossibility to mourn, as though to enable the gaping [*déhiscence*] of the object, of which a part is somehow unlost.

Thus, anxiety arises not when loss is revealed, but when the Other's impossibility to yield, to cede, returns to the subject to an unbearable degree. In other words, anxiety as a stopgap registers the recognition of an absence of lack.[2] During analysis this time should be recognized as especially fruitful, and it demands great watchfulness on the part of the analyst, who must never lose sight that the analysand's life is in danger.

To establish something that can be given up—this, then, is one of the functions of anxiety. This function, considering the place that Lacan assigns it in the [Freudian] sequence "inhibition-symptom-anxiety," is the product of the effects of the imaginary inhibition on the one hand and of embarrassment and commotion located in the register of the Real, on the other.[3]

This Real[4] is represented by the eruption of the Other as the subject comes into existence. To illustrate this hypothesis, Lacan

---

[2] Lacan, speaking of *his anxiety*, prompted by the parroting [psittacism] of psychoanalysts, would cry out "I'm lacking lack!" (Anxiety seminar, Strasbourg congress, École freudienne de Paris, 1976).

[3]

LINE OF GREATEST DIFFICULTY

	IMAGINARY	SYMBOLIC	REAL
IMAGINARY	Inhibition	Hindrance	Embarrassment
SYMBOLIC	Emotion	Symptom	*Passage à l'acte*
REAL	Commotion	Acting out	Anxiety

Table drawn up by Jean Allouch, Diane Chauvelot, Jacques Hassoun, Philippe Julien, André Rondepierre, study group (Anxiety seminar, Strasbourg congress, École freudienne de Paris, 1976).

[4] Let us recall that the Real is not reality. It could be represented by that sequence in Ingmar Bergman's *Cries and Whispers* in which the protagonists are called upon to express themselves in a language foreign to all other languages to convey the climate of strangeness in which they all are steeped.

offers the image of the child who comes into the world with a cry. Trauma, he says, is not the sign of separation from the mother; it signifies the breathing into itself—and "aspiration in itself"—of this essentially Other environment into which the child finds himself projected. Living, he breathes in this surrounding air, aspires to— the Other and separates himself from it; he exists. Now this Real, so presented in anxiety, accounts for the eruption of an affect that attests to a lack "of air" able at times to become opaque and inaudible.

"I'm the one missing from the *jouissance* of the Other." This would be the impossible sentence (an impossible formulation that signals the Real) giving the anxiety-ridden person the dreadful mission of sustaining the enigmatic desire of the Other. To explain myself better, let me come back once more to passion: If in general "what is desired is the desiring of the Other," in passion the sole source for desire is the impassioned person, no one else. Which is why that person asks: "What object, cause of desire, am I for this desire that I have created from scratch, a desire I impute to the other and which in fact creates me?" This questioning may represent a way of filling in the lack of *jouissance* that the impassioned person lends to the other. One mission and one mission only seems to be entrusted by the impassioned person to the being who has caused his passion: to reveal and confirm, by the resistance he offers, that perfect coincidence is useless, that communication is impossible, and that the desire-causing object is lost from the start. Isn't it this delegating that rouses the impassioned person's despair and accounts for the spill he takes the moment the passion breaks down, becoming the melancholia he has tried to ward off in yielding to this *mise en abyme?*

It is here that passion and erotomania differ radically. In the first case, there is something of the other—a haphazard, anonymous, other—generally taken aback at having been chosen, but who may or may not take to this passion, keep subjectivity, and, steering a middle course, maintain a position as desiring subject. Whereas in the latter case, the renamed/renowned other [*re-nommé*] (in order to be eventually denominated [*dénommé*]) is too subjugated by the erotomaniac for hatred not to emerge.

Lacan points out that if the formula of desire, as it is determined by the first object, is written D (*a*)[5] in anxiety, the first object, *a*, is replaced by the anxiety. At this point, he adds, the formula for anxiety might also be written D (*a*), but here the object *a*—cause of desire—is substituted by anxiety, which is characteristically object-less. This means that the victim of this disorder is prey to the dreadful horror of an objectless desire. Such would be a first approach to Lacan's statement: anxiety, which has no cause, is the search for an object. Passion—the key site of anxious waiting— offers a remarkable illustration of this statement. Indeed, the being who so rouses the impassioned person is robbed of all otherness. He can be viewed more or less as a hook for these fragments of objects salvaged from a wreck, waiting, it would seem, for some imaginary recipient who might allow them to cause desire. So the impassioned person has eyes only for the man or woman ostensibly equipped with these drive objects. He lives only for hearing his or her voice, and forms a consuming relationship with him or her; and nothing, it seems, can put out this flash-fire. Rashly enough this passion-causing being is expected to establish itself as a desire-causing object in order to allow the impassioned person to pull himself out of melancholic destitution.[6] The impassioned person lives like a nursling, waiting for some marvel to occur, in wait for some sudden halt to the drift of affects, waiting for the chance to reach the other, who would have slipped off with what has adorned him or her.

For, let there be no mistake: impassioned people love some anonymous and perfectly indifferent person burdened with representing the enigma of which they find themselves the victim. One

---

5 Jacques Lacan, notation on *désir de l'objet cause de désir* [desire of the desire-causing object] (Anxiety seminar, Strasbourg congress, École freudienne de Paris, 1976).

6 Let us recall that in passion the desire-causing object, highly mobile, and thoroughly nonreflective, is affixed, molded, onto the body of her or him who rouses the passion, who will then be merged with it.

need only recall, in summary, the apologia with which Lacan opens his seminar on anxiety: "Masked, the subject does not know with what eyes the 'praying mantis' sees him . . . she cannot be named . . . and were she to name herself, he would not be able to hear her, since he does not know whom she sees, to whom she addresses herself, and finally what she wants of him. And it is because he does not know what she wants of him—*che vuoi?* [What do you want?]—that he cannot do without her."

The need, the necessity even of being present to the Other in the absence of all knowledge, fulfills the condition of the wait that a mythical servility constantly maintains.

Such a wait must be situated in the radical absence of pulsation, rhythm, play of absence-and-presence, that marks the return to the Real of the nontransferable. For someone in thrall to it, the anxious wait is the nucleus of a long discontinuity—a troubled, crippling inertia—corresponding, in the table Lacan gives us in his Anxiety seminar, to the intersection of greatest embarrassment or perturbation (*l'embarras*) and greatest commotion (*l'émoi*).[7]

Everything about the progress of a passion, in all its exemplariness, points to this turmoil, this drift, as the courtly expression of anxiety: from the time of the encounter to the dénouement ("from time immemorial" to "nevermore") we are confronted with the passage of desire insofar as it is determined by the first object and with desire as it is determined by the first anxiety. This wait, puzzling in itself, translates the surprise of the thunderbolt and upsets the dialectic of demand and desire to stage and direct the order of need, which relates to what Cocteau referred to as the reign of negative despotism.

Isn't this negative despotism the end point and key to the subject's anxious wait, repeating his failure to be, in order to send him scuttling toward that which beckons in the Other? Identified with some perpetually lacking trait, the subject hovers between perplexity and misunderstanding. This lacking trait that has obsessed him

---

reveals how worn out the blind Imaginary is that's sustained his passion: on the Symbolic side, it indicates the disconnecting of a signifier, and on the Real side, what results from a failed inscription and the radical impotence the subject has faced.

If for Lacan the wait is the signal for anxiety, impotence for Freud is at the origin of anxiety as a signal. This impotence makes the passionate person a prisoner who, bound hand and foot, finds himself at the mercy of the opaque desire of the being with whom he is in love (or in love-hate)[8]; for ultimately this desire is the echo of his own. In fact, if passion stages and enacts a radical asymmetry, it likewise unveils the impassioned person's desire to submit to an Other who has total authority over his life, including the power of death. The anxious wait of the impassioned person in the grips of disastrous defeat lies between incessant pain and the impossibility of emptying or diverting in any way whatsoever the tension that racks him and that renders ineffectual any reaction from the pleasure principle. This defeat seals the process of unbinding drives.

The exalted bond of passion is sustained by an Imaginary situated in a Beyond of desire. We can envision it as an eye searching its own depths for the absent image of the ideal Ego offered up to the other, who withholds it. This explains the assertion that the signal of anxiety relates to an object that perturbs (Lacan's word) the ideal Ego, which originates in the specular Ego. The mirror image in anxiety thus ceases to be sustained by the Other: the mirror is definitely empty, and the wait is that of an image that only the other's vision, voice, caress can attempt to restore in a split second, while, as with Dorian Gray, the restored image will remain constantly alien, between eternal youth and premature decline: "It's never that." And the loved object is always on the verge of being lost.

This internal, drive-related pain attests to an extreme difficulty and an apathy that prompts Freud to remark that any effort at movement, in the case of melancholia, proves ineffectual. The pain

---

[8] [*hainamourré*: a pun mixing *énamouré* with *haine* (hate), with an echo of the *mor(r)a* explained previously. Trans.]

of waiting corresponds to the powerlessness to regain an image to which impassioned persons find themselves subjugated, and that melancholics rediscover in a time of remission in which they discover the abyss into which they've plunged.

Thus the wait, which functions as an anxiety signal, is the means for maintaining "the relation to desire" in the very place where desire seems to be lacking. In this regard, desire as a remedy to anxiety represents an exit from stasis and inertia, which represents the triumph of a deadly Real entrapping the impassioned person to the point of troubling embarrassment [*embarras*]. Waiting, capturing, passion in its disastrous aspect, flight, distress, insurmountable anguish—all are restagings of the various forms of identification but also of the investment of the Other by the ideal Ego, and quite peculiarly so: the Other is required to take the place of the ideal Ego to a point of total coincidence, of "standing in for" or doubling.

There are two ways to read this doubling: the other whom the impassioned one depicts to himself as being at the origins of his passion is object of a summoning. He is called upon to say in behalf of the passion-ridden person what the latter cannot articulate. What befalls him seems so strange, so alien to his life, that his discourse seems to need—in order to become audible—subtitles, without which it would become incomprehensible to everyone, himself included.

Now, beings reputed to have unleashed such a passion are, at the same time, forever suspected of doubling for those they've impassioned. They're apt to be suspected always of producing nothing but lying, inaudible words. Their existence produces waiting and anxiety from the moment of the first encounter, when some feature detached from the whole will represent the totality of these beings. This element will be the source of further anxiety to the very extent that it is disclosed as a nontransferable object, one that has never awaited an encounter. In this regard, the encounter with the beloved being reveals the wait for something magical. The assumption of *being object of passion* in behalf of the desire-causing object marks the horror felt by subjects made passive by this endless wait, which will later plunge them into melancholia. At the end of a passion no bargain has been struck, and nothing's been got round: detachment from the object can be as sudden, as brutal as the encounter itself was. This fall can occur in two ways:

- either in the form of dejection—the sort Proust describes in the very last lines of *Swann's Way [Swann in Love]*: "And with the old, intermittent caddishness which reappeared in him when he was no longer unhappy and his moral standards dropped accordingly, he exclaimed to himself: 'To think that I've wasted years of my life, that I've longed to die, that I've experienced my greatest love, for a woman who didn't appeal to me, who wasn't even my type!' "[9] Whereas the poet Marina Tsvetayava sends the man packing from her life with these words: "To love is to see a man as God conceived him, and as his parents did not make him. Not to love is to see the man as his parents made him. To no longer love is to see in his place a table, a chair;"[10]
- or it can occur in the form of melancholia in which the remorse felt by the subjects tortured by the ending of some lacerating passion reveals the "suicide of the object" of which they have, unwillingly, been the agent.

Now, if the object's suicide represents a radical assault on subjectivity, anxiety, in turn, attests to the maintenance of a desire that tends to show that the anxiety neither has a cause nor could be a cause. Having reached this end point, we can also state that melancholics who have stopped waiting for anything know anxiety only in those moments of remission when their state improves to the

---

[9] Marcel Proust, *Swann's Way*, vol. 1 of *Remembrance of Things Past*, trans. C. K. Scott Moncrieff and Terence Kilmartin (New York: Vintage Books, 1982), 415; *Un Amour de Swann*, vol. 1 of *À la recherche du temps perdu. Du côté de chez Swann* (Paris: GF-Flammarion, 1987).

[10] Marina Tsvetaeva, *Neuf lettres avec une dixième retenue et une onzième reçue* (Paris: Clémence Hiver, 1985).

point at which, faced with a causeless, deadly desire, they may hurtle themselves deathward, toward the final fall.[11]

To shift waiting[12] into the framework of the melancholics' treatment may represent their first moment of having access to desire. It's a matter, then, of immediately grasping the anxiety signal in order to help the analysand pull away from the tyranny of an unlost object, an object that is cause of nothing, the distant offshoot of a maternal love that should have been the cause of everything.

---

[11] Clinical experience teaches us that death by defenestration may be the resolution of an anxiety crisis during the melancholic's "remission" period.

[12] In the treatment of melancholics the rhythm and time of sessions should not, for instance, suffer the least "manipulation." It is crucial, in fact, to hold firmly to course safely round every bend by refraining, that is (and let us stress this), from shortening or extending the time of sessions, much less altering their rhythm. It is in this framework, i.e., *into* the transference, that the time of the wait can be shifted.

Chapter 6

"I would prefer not to"

HOW DOES ONE CONJURE UP the suspension of desire, the imprisonment in death, the bliss and cruelty of the endless litany delivered to the other and to oneself, how does one envision this staging of a mute protest? How does one speak of the stupor, the listlessness, the desubjectivization, the passive resistance that aims at a supreme victory over the other even at the cost of self-destruction? How does one address this time in which the paths of drives all seem blocked, clamped into place, one after the other, as in some disaster script, so that a living person's functions seem to drop to mere need and survival? Melancholia, which tends to attack what is vital in the Other, surrounds and cancerously gnaws at those in the patient's immediate circle, engulfing them finally in a feeling of passive beatitude.

"Nothing is plenty for me," such is the formula, repeated and heard a thousand times, of an extreme satiety whereby, for want of lack, it suddenly seems inconceivable that there could be any opening that might lead out to the channels of pleasure. The melancholic's world is one of asthmatic suffocation, of forbidden song, of untimely music, of a gaze opening onto a hallucination of absence, anorexia, retention, blank death.

The image that would best suit the melancholic's talk would be that of a walled, rock-laden fortress standing guard before some horrible desert where nothing ever happens, no event could or should occur, under pain of prompting a disorder that might reveal the original nature of this ostensibly impregnable castle. All enticement from without damages, destroys, levels to their final form—in a dazed atmosphere of bewilderment—those melancholics groaning under the weight of a repletion absence has planted in them. This assumption has led us to state that melancholics are people who have not known the experience of a loss and of an initial subjectivizing mourning process; not that they have been engulfed in a maternal desire that would make them psychotic, quite the contrary, they have been desperately filled up; desperately, that is to say, abjectly. Something has been sacrificed in them but nothing has been given to them. The gift, that is the loss of the other in the Other, has not been able to manifest itself for them. They have not been able to reach this stage: nor can they get over this impossibility.

At which point, the melancholic, having become a *man without quality,* without recognition, sinks into apathy. He no longer expects anything. He stands poised and firm in the course of time, which he halts by his very presence, neither dead nor alive, neither desiring nor absorbed in any passion whatsoever; the melancholic lives the extreme cruelty that the world exerts upon him as the expression of a logic radically alien to him, to which he responds by an other logic: the cryptic one of his inert cruelty. Ferocity comprises a strange mix of rejection, worry, and fascination felt toward the other, who then cannot help but let himself be seized by this force of inertia that's content to have nothing, that even tries to find this relieving nothing in order to open a breach in the repletion of a laughable completeness.

Though bursting to the gills, melancholics never stop sententiously proclaiming their decline, their decrepitude, their destitution: yet even as they utter them, these words are like terms pulled from some foreign language they are struggling to understand or make palpable. Faced with the impossibility of speaking of their extreme indigence and meagerness, melancholics will go to the point of inventing, through neologisms, a language able to account for this ruinous overfullness. This is why they can inspire painters, musicians, novelists, or essayists, who acknowledge them as exemplars of the fate of humanity gripped by an impossible bereavement, by silences that are essentially withholdings, by unspoken crimes that remain to be carried out and must therefore be constantly repeated.[1] Writers like Dostoyevsky, Blanchot, or Thomas Bernhard have seen this quite clearly: the melancholic possesses a knowledge about a society that seems unable to live unless it has scapegoats, whose sacrifice nonetheless derives from a radical failure of inscription. He can inspire only narrations without fiction, so great seems the lack, even in the case of his own writings, caught in endless rehearsals, of what gives writing its gravity: the margin. For if this margin graphically represents the breathing space, the place where the Other—as reader—is called upon to seize upon the text in order to write down his reflections, his graffiti, his manifestations of life, his interpretations, then we can conceive of a melancholic's story as a sentence with no possible appeal [in the judicial sense]: he's condemned in advance and the Other will always fall this side of the verdict. He is his own cop, his own jailer, his own hangman: as such, out of reach. He is the other's castoff, his dregs, and reveals to this other his own decay.

This position of fearsome resistance in inertia is disheartening. Like a passion, it is also nonnegotiable. And it can, perhaps, inspire only those works condemned to stage nothing but the sheer intransigence of an impossible desire.

To illustrate my point, I want to discuss Melville's tale "Bartleby."[2]

Bartleby is [a young man] employed as a copyist, a scrivener, who one day, when his boss—a lawyer, and the narrator—asks him to collate legal texts that he and his fellow scriveners have been copying, replies: "I would prefer not to." Gradually, from this moment

---

[1] A good example of this occurs in Roman Polanski's film, *The Tenant* (1976).

[2] Herman Melville, "Bartleby," in *Billy Budd and Other Stories* (New York: Penguin Books, 1986). Cf. Anne Longuet-Marx, "Bartleby, allégorie d'une vanité," *Apertura*, 10:(in press).

on, this *I would prefer not to* will infect first all of Bartleby's activities, then those of the workers in the office, who one after another take up variants of the phrase: all start to *prefer* or *prefer not,* something unheard-of in this austere Wall Street lawyer's office, in which Bartleby will install himself, live, sleep. One day his boss—whom one hardly expects to show such benevolence toward an employee—surprises this strange occupant:

> Upon more closely examining the place, I surmised that for an indefinite period Bartleby must have eaten, dressed, and slept in my office, and that, too without plate, mirror, or bed. The cushioned seat of a rickety old sofa in one corner bore the faint impress of a lean, reclining form. Rolled away under his desk, I found a blanket; under the empty grate, a blacking box and brush; on a chair, a tin basin, with soap and a ragged towel; in a newspaper a few crumbs of ginger-nuts and a morsel of cheese. Yes, thought I, it is evident enough that Bartleby has been making his home here, keeping bachelor's hall all by himself.[3]

Henceforth, the situation will become so intolerable that the lawyer, after having tried to reason with Bartleby, goes to the lengths of suggesting he take a vacation or serve as tutor to a young man from a good family, all the while eliciting only a blank gaze and the same response, "I would prefer not to"; in fact, he is doomed to give ground to this strange character, moving surreptitiously to the other end of Wall Street. Yet this intruder, living in extreme penury, continues to fascinate the narrator to the point that the latter forgoes the chance to learn his secret. On his visit to what has become Bartleby's residence, the lawyer [finding a key in the lock to "Bartleby's closed desk"] discovers a "savings bank." He does not open it. He will keep intact the mystery surrounding Bartleby's past. The melancholic venom is all too present. It would be ridiculous to bring to light what might in any way represent elements that might reconstitute any sort of fiction, the fleeting trace of a past life.

---

[3] Melville, "Bartleby," 22.

This savings bank, hidden in a bandana in a closed but unlocked desk, discovered and left inviolate, is the real secret of this work.[4] It represents the futility of any objectivization of the melancholic's reality, his potentialities, his history. There remains only Bartleby, who will end his days in a prison he has wished upon himself. Ever under the influence, fascinated by his inertia, his apathy, the narrator gives money to the prison's so-called *grub-man* to try to improve the daily fare of one whose incarceration has driven him to the ultimate state of "preferring not to." Bartleby will end his days letting himself die of hunger, presenting the world with a form of insurmountable resistance that nothing and no one could overcome.[5]

Is Bartleby's "I would prefer not to" the melancholic equivalent of the motto *"Je résisterai"* [I shall resist/endure. Trans.] that the Huguenot prisoner Marie Durand carved in stone in her prison cell? Is it the expression of the violence of a puritanism disappointed with an America of already dashed ideals? Might it be the catastrophic trace of Melville's stint, between two sea voyages, in a New York law firm in 1840? Isn't it simply the logical outcome of Captain Ahab's quest: Ahab who, dominated by his passion to encounter that wondrous object—the white whale—inscribes his life in the quest for an impossible desire? Isn't it, above all, that confrontation with the *too late* that the living person, Bartleby, can encounter only when overwhelmed by an impossibile grief? This too late, already so before the encounter has even been set in place, has nothing to do with a refusal of action: it has to do, rather, with an

---

4 Neither Blanchot, nor Deleuze, nor Anne Longuet-Marx has pointed out the importance of this inviolate bank.

5 At the end of the tale, only after the narrator has learned of his death, it is revealed that Bartleby formerly worked as "a subordinate clerk" in the Dead Letter Office, constantly confronted with the "too late" inherent in the melancholic's existence: "Sometimes from out the folded paper the pale clerk takes a ring—the finger it was meant for, perhaps, moulders in the grave; a bank-note sent in swiftest charity—he whom it would relieve, nor eats nor hungers any more; pardon for those who died despairing; hope for those who died unhoping; good tidings for those who died stifled by unrelieved calamities. [On errands of life, these letters speed to death.]" Melville, "Bartleby," 46.

act that precedes the ending and places the subject out of reach of the other's aggressivity or violence. Everything is already accomplished even before the binding of life drives and death drives could inscribe what makes the living person a desiring subject.

But if we've been able to make the assumption that the melancholic founders where the paranoiac succeeds in failing, we have to know at what place the analyst first manages to treat melancholics. The analyst succeeds when he puts into play his own desire as it has taken shape in the moment when the analysand's treatment has taken a didactic turn. It is during this time when the analysand, on his way to becoming the analyst, comes closest to pure desire, desire for that which, being veiled, establishes lack as a category, but which at the same time proves to be beyond the signified. This virtual yet inaugural time is that in which this analysand seems to encounter the *Thing,* at the very instant it's being taken over for by the desire-causing object.

From what is represented of the inscription of the death drive in the Ego, an intervention in the treatments of melancholics—faced as they are with the never perpetrated murder and required always to renew the primal object—can function as a signifying cut and enable the joint work of creation, sublimation, and horror that characterizes the psychoanalytical act in its extreme. It is from the very place of passage through death, the place of this *passe,* that the analyst can—in the transference—intervene in treatment of melancholia.[6]

I am reminded here of another figure of cruelty prompted by the technicized violence of the concentration camp world, transforming the deportees into *Musulmänner* doomed to push *preferring not to* to its limit. Of those suicides who one day cheated the hangman out of their death, Primo Levi writes:

> Whosoever does not know how to become an *Organisator, Kombinator, Prominent* (the savage eloquence of these words!) soon

---

6 This is how today we understand the timely intervention that completely shifts the progress of the deep melancholia Roxane was bogging down in.

becomes a "mussulman." In life a third way exists, and is in fact the rule: it does not exist in the concentration camp.

To sink is the easiest of matters; it is enough to carry out all the orders one receives, to eat only the ration, to observe the discipline of the work and the camp. Experience showed that only exceptionally could one survive more than three months in this way. All the mussulmans who finished in the gas chambers have the same story; they followed the slope down to the bottom, like streams that run down to the sea. On their entry into the camp, through basic incapacity, or by misfortune, or through some banal incident, they are overcome before they can adapt themselves; they are beaten by time, they do not begin to learn German, to disentangle the infernal knot of laws and prohibitions until their bodies are already in decay, and nothing can save them from selection or from death by exhaustion. Their life is short, but their number is endless. They, the *Musulmänner,* the drowned, form the backbone of the camp: an anonymous mass, continually renewed and always identical, of "non-men" who march and labor in silence, the divine spark dead within them, already too empty to really suffer. One hesitates to call them living. One hesitates to call their death death, in the face of which they have no fear, as they are too tired to understand.[7]

This raises a hypothesis I don't venture without some apprehension, for its sheer indecency: These benighted *Musulmänner* embodied the real truth of the camps: the regimentation, the rationed food, the nonexistent disease prevention, could lead only to death: the death that was already there. Didn't some of these *Musulmänner* kill themselves with it, in order to die of inner death?[8]

---

[7] Primo Levi, *Survival in Auschwitz,* trans. Stuart Woolf (New York: Collier Books, 1961), 81–82. I counter this attitude with that of the suicides in the camps who hurled themselves against the electrified barbed wire to bring about their deaths. Speaking of them, Germaine Tillon in *Ravensbruck* (Paris: Le Seuil, 1988) cites a dialogue: to a woman deportee who attempted to end her life in this way, he raised the argument (one which would bear fruit): "If you do that, you won't know the end of the story." Disillusioned, the *Musulmann* is only too certain of the end of the story (at least as far as he is concerned).

[8] Sigmund Freud, in *Beyond the Pleasure Principle,* hypothesizes that "Every living being necessarily dies of internal causes."

Is the same process at work in the resistance the indigenous peoples of the Caribbean put up to the arrival of missionaries and slave traders to their islands, letting themselves die without descendants? Can we categorize such a process as a sort of applied melancholia? Here we come up against the undecidable, all the more so because this form of (non-)resistance tips the living over into the realm of the funereal, turning that topological figure of the Moebius strip, so that at the end of a final reversion, death and life reconjoin, their functions taking on equal weight.

If institutions tend to maintain themselves by driving the object to suicide, if they try to live only on that margin while denying it, if power leaves that much less space for play—i.e., for the dialectic of gift giving and loss—so that it grows more dictatorial, we can venture this assumption: that the more a power rests upon enthusiasm, once the first phases of impassioned and fascinated devotion are over (and what is a passion but a defense against melancholy?), the likelier it is to produce a second phase, one of apathy, of a waiting deemed pointless in advance, and of impossible mourning for an enigmatic loss.

One figure of this apathy toward power could be represented by the young Jakob von Gunten,[9] who leaves his family in mysterious circumstances to enter the Benjamenta Institute where "one learns very little," but where what is taught to the pupils will allow them "later to be meek and humble people."

Whereas Bartleby uses and abuses his "I would prefer not to" in order to cut short every demand coming from the other, Jakob von Gunten never stops slavishly saying "I'd be happy to do it," although when instructed to provide a curriculum vitae, he takes an eternity to prepare it[10]: never satisfied with the description he gives of the

---

[9] Robert Walser, *Jakob von Gunten*, English trans. *Institute Benjamenta*, trans. Christopher Middleton (London: Serpent's Tail Press, 1995).

[10] It is often remarked that melancholics have an extremely hard time drawing up the biographical or bio-bibliographic elements that force them to take stock of the path they've taken, to gauge their own *worth*.

course of his life, he will never be sufficiently humble to express the vast pride that fills him. Answering Mr. Benjamenta, who tells him of his intentions to find him an exceptional position worthy of his rank, young Jacob will exclaim:

> "Exception? I make no exceptions. That is not fitting for the son of an alderman. My modesty, my birth, all my feelings forbid me to wish for more than what my fellow-pupils have received."[11]

So, at the end of this desperate tale, Jacob, musing on the life unfolding for him, sets to thinking:

> And if I am smashed to pieces and go to ruin, what is being smashed and ruined? A zero. The individual me is only a zero. . . . I'm going with Herr Benjamenta into the desert.[12]

In the desert, he will be able to suspend his existence and, like an anchorite, think of nothing more.

> Not even of God? No! God will be with me. What should I need to think of Him? God goes with thoughtless people.[13]

He doesn't think. He sheds his subjectivity, rids himself of his thought, his desire in that interior desert he wishes upon himself, the desert of this *happy to do it* that anticipates the other's demand, and—superego-like—will plunge him into extreme melancholic *jouissance* to the point of resisting before whatever would divert him from his apathy has even occurred. Before the fact he is ready to accept everything in order to safeguard the linguistic enclave that is neither a yes nor a no, but a resigned acceptance, a blend of negativism, inertia, and resistance.

Melancholic subjection faces the impossibility of language

---

[11] Walser, *Institute Benjamenta*, p. 133.

[12] Ibid., p. 136.

[13] Ibid.

expressing resignation. This impasse leads us to ask whether melancholic apathy can represent a resistance to power tending toward dictatorship or totalitarianism, as we have suggested with the example of the *Musulmänner*. We might well think so, provided we forget that this apathy eludes the subject: only paradoxically is it an act of passive resistance; in fact, in overwhelming the subject it reveals the inner cruelty that afflicts him and the responses that ensue (*I would prefer not to/I'd be happy to do it*) are then only the last jaculations that, prior to psychic death, attempt to formulate a fast-fading desire.

As I've mentioned, if the formula for desire is determined by the desire of the first object, if it is the nature of the first object to be lost in melancholia and the troubled, crippling inertia that characterizes it before it finally founders, then every object roused externally—even an esthetic object—can be constituted as an object of violence wielded toward the subject. This subject risks then falling into the representation of an inability to mourn. In other circumstances the object is called upon to arouse anxiety, which Lacan relates to desire as it is determined by the first anxiety—that is, by a causeless object, a nearly object, a not-entirely object, like the the air the newborn child breathes, which is traumatic only insofar as it attests to the manifestation of the Other's existence in that newborn's body.

The melancholic, then—mouth, genitals, and anus sealed, erotic body sealed—may be hurtled toward a destruction—defenestration in particular—by which he stages the fall of that fallout, that trash his body represents. Yet anxiety also may contribute—quite precisely, in this instance—to creating a work of art, a piece of writing, music that will express the recoil in which the melancholic has shut himself, in which his partial drives, far from following out their winding course, clamp down upon themselves. If ever there's a time of resistance, a manifestation of life in the melancholic's petrified world, it comes when anxiety reveals itself as capable of creating a desire-causing object.

Certainly anxiety can in its own way be crippling. Yet however little the subject encounters here of the signifying chain, an object—anxiety provoking but able to replace the *not to* in the

formula *I would prefer not to*—will then be able to sever the subject
from its *jouissance*, its subjection, its apathy, to allow it to pry itself
out of its decrepitude and to recognize that an Other exists. The
surrogate object may be represented by a word, but just as well by a
few notes from some forgotten melody, some lines from a once-
heard poem, some furtive caresses light as a bird's feather, which
might chime with the submerged, mired, stuck fragments in this
part of the first object that escaped loss. Access to this object comes
from the creation, the effort to call into existence the Other denied
by the melancholic; it comes from a return to affects such as fright or
anxiety, able to destabilize resistences built upon quicksand, to allow
for the binding of drives and the advent of desire. In these circumstances, the analyst's desire is summoned to an interpretation that
serves as creation. The emergence of this sheer creation, an emer-
gency exit for the melancholic, would, in the social order, contain
the political act capable of shaking the cowed apathy[14] of those who
risk identifying themselves with the image of trash they're offered
through an Ego Ideal. The act that shatters passivity, issuing from the
very place of anxiety, allows for the emergence of the living being's
desire. This is also the time when certain acts of resistance without
great military importance (such as the revolt of the Warsaw Ghetto
or the saga of the Man[o]uchian-Boczow group) have been able to
represent not just a leap but a true breach, true discovery; it's the
moment when a *Guernica* gets painted, *L'Honneur des poètes*[15] gets
written, a time of regaining a long lost subjectivity.

---

14 It is obvious that when a society is founded upon the savagery of what (or who) rouses
the desire of subjects the better to drive them to suicide, the institutions that knit together
the body social seem to hold only in the empty word of a Master, whose slogan would
be "One alone can speak or think in the name of all." Here the dialectic that governs
exchange, loss, and gift giving is withdrawn in favor of sacrifice (the one demanded of
the subjugated, vaunted for "making a gift of one's person to the State, to the group, the
institution") and of melancholy, which now takes pride of place in the "discontent" that
invades a "civilization."

15 [A collection of Resistance poetry, ed. Paul Éluard (Éditions de Minuit, 1945). Trans.]

Chapter 7

The Black Sun of Melancholy

MANIA MANIFESTS ITSELF by the feeling of boundless potency, reckless levity, language mastery, full hypermnesia; it's the display of an existence dominated by the limitless. Now the universe of melancholics—which on first sight strikes us as narrow, cramped, shrunken, bleak to the point of making them almost aphasic—nonetheless faces the same absence of limits. This terrifying limitlessness is that of a world in which the object is nowhere to be found. The baffling absence of what cannot be represented, of what has failed to present itself, can only underscore the lack of markers and relay points, the impossibility of a boundary line that greets melancholics on a daily basis. For this reason their world will be dominated by a huge resentment which, like a cancer, invades their existence with its metastasis: unaware of what insult has been dealt them and what they lack, they barely even know how to envision what failed to occur; so in the long, slow monologue they lock themselves into, they will spin out harangues that are at once aggrieved and cruel.

The clamor for redress does not correspond perfectly, despite a certain resemblance, to the paranoiac's cantankerousness; it aims at a wrong whose exact parameters are blurred. Some ghastly, deplorable thing always keeps happening to melancholics, yet nothing in their history allows them to see what might have marked them out as particularly unworthy.

Having neither outline nor form, this puzzling catastrophe presumably could never become an object of narration, much less fiction. It is fit only for endless rehearsal: every event, whether ordinary or exceptional, takes its inevitable turn for the worse, contains the reminder that an unjust and cruel fate besets the one whose inner universe is invaded by *black bile*. Everything in this person conspires to form this feeling, and nothing, it seems, can create a preserve for play, for sport of any sort that might cheer the existence of this perpetual bereavement.

We find an illustration of this grayish universe in Kafka's story "The Hunter Gracchus"[1]: Gracchus, pursuing a chamois one day in the Black Forest, falls off a cliff. Ever after, he drifts in a bark that cannot cross the river separating the dead from the living, a bark that takes him from town to town.

"Since then I have been dead."

"But you are alive too," said the Burgomaster.

"In a certain sense," said the hunter, "in a certain sense I am alive too. My death ship lost its way; a wrong turn of the wheel, a moment's absence of mind on the pilot's part, a longing to turn aside toward my lovely native country, I cannot tell what it was; I only know this, that I remained on earth and that ever since my ship has sailed earthly waters. So I, who asked for nothing better than to live among my mountains, travel after my death through all the lands of the earth."[2]

"Nobody will read what I say here, no one will come to help me; even if all the people were commanded to help me, every door and window would remain shut, everybody would take to bed and draw the bedclothes over his head, the whole earth would become an inn for the night. And there is sense in that, for nobody knows of me, and if anyone knew, he would not know where I could be found, and if he knew where I could be found, he would not know how to deal with

---

1 Franz Kafka, *Selected Short Stories*, trans. Willa and Edwin Muir (New York: The Modern Library, 1993), 191–198.

2 Kafka, "The Hunter Gracchus," 194–195.

me, he would not know how to help me. The thought of helping me is an illness that has to be cured by taking to one's bed. I know that, and so I do not shout to summon help, even though at moments when I lose control over myself, as I have done just now, for instance, I think seriously of it."[3]

Nothing and no one can help him. Wouldn't anyone who did have such a strange idea need bed rest at least, wouldn't he simply share his listlessness, and—why not?—take his place as the living dead, an eternal wanderer lost in some immemorial nonplace?

For melancholics seem to possess no memory that does not concern the sad lot they suffer. All the erratic fragments of a selective reminiscence seem to cluster around this prior sentence whose ultimate form is the feeling of suffering a punishment; they shut melancholics in a dim universe of nonlife and nondeath. None of their memories seems able to organize itself around recollection, and no construction—which, in analysis, can at times have an effect of interpretation in filling in excised parts of a hidden family history—can form an alternative to their pain and suffering.

The futility of any attempt to reorganize this wounded memory and thus wrest it from its inertia is likely to disarm the psychoanalyst, whose untimely intervention risks a stinging reply: "You know how deprived I am. No pain is like the pain I feel, and your efforts to console me are no help whatsoever."

Though mindful of how chancy such an assumption can be, we are led to ask ourselves: Can't we detect in certain psychic breakdowns of presenescence (accompanied by an amnesia that affects the past as well as the present) a melancholic amnesia dominated entirely by a static hypermnesia, which eventually seems to resolve into amnesia?

Reading Pierre Pachet's remarkable work, *Autobiographie de mon père*,[4] lends some support to this assumption: Pierre Pachet will

---

[3] Ibid., 197.

[4] Pierre Pachet, *Autobiographie de mon père* (Autobiography of my father) (Paris: Autrement-Littératures, 1994).

gradually let his father, Simkha Apatchevsky (or Opatchevsky), have his say and reestablish his history so that his memory helps him to write it. The tone is set from the start:

> My mother died when I was five. I cannot help the fact that her disappearance would be the determining fact of my life, or that, however far back in time it took place, it would lose none of its terrible force. People who talk with me often fault me for one character trait or another, refusing to see that I have no control over the essential one, by force of circumstance. And in a sense, when I say that for me my mother's death seems to have happened just yesterday, I'm not exaggerating: the downfall it marked is the sort that cannot be filled and . . . it condemned me to utter irrevocability.[5]

He doesn't remember his mother's features, but rather her love:

> Don't laugh: what remains of her for me is precisely what I never found later on, a love that is undivided, and the certainty, though I no longer know if I'm remembering correctly or imagining it, of being the favorite. This is a statement of sheer good sense, yet I have constantly to remind those close to me who, thank God, have not known this heartbreak: it makes a difference to have or not have your mother.[6]

The narrator's history is completely dominated by this intrusive, seemingly insurmountable grief.

He emigrates from Russia, settles in France, attends university, marries, becomes the father of two children, survives the First World War, escapes deportation during the Second. From the look of things, then, his family, social, and professional life has been a success. Deep down, though, he lives in the bitter certainty that his existence is stamped with failure. Fate has always dealt harshly with him, not because the grass is always greener on the other side, but because there has never been and never will be grass:

---

5 Ibid., 11.

6 Ibid., 11–12.

The sun was dazzling, I had to put a pair of smoked protective lenses over my glasses, but they kept slipping off and ended up blinding me almost totally, except for a few rare unscreened glances I managed to steal, but those were crowned with full success, giving me access to . . . an infinitely remote, fleeting world which one stole into only surreptitiously.[7]

With his frightening lucidity, he is better able than anyone, even when the blank psychosis of his inner disaster gains ground, to analyze Hitler's success with the masses and to spot Evil at work in the social realm. It is then that, gradually divested of the last bit of eroticism that kept him in life, he clearheadedly attempts to describes his state:

Why is it that no one I know can put up with the discontinuity I live in? Why is it that the rare encounters I still have force me to fake, between states of consciousness, a bond I no longer feel?[8]

Or this description, before calling up some of his childhood recollections:

I'm scared of death, of suffering in solitude, of the bed you don't leave alive, strangers hovering overhead, their gazes wandering over the bed like flies. In our homes the dying would recite psalms, with occasional singing of the *Shema Israel* as a kind of refrain you should have on your lips at the last moment, since you never know when the last moment will come, a sort of rehearsal of last rites you administer yourself. Curious. I'm not really scared of death, only of incorrigible stupidity.[9]

A confirmed misanthrope, devoted utterly to a nameless sorrow, an immense bitterness, the narrator slowly but surely sees his moor-

---

[7] Ibid., 105–106.

[8] Ibid., 116.

[9] Ibid., 119–120.

ings seized from him, with no rupture marking the disaster that's befallen him. Still, though, when he enters into the last phase of his existence, he's unable to approach death but only the world of the alien. Indeed, the very term *death,* which has dominated his entire existence, has always been too separate, too detached from the signifer *mourning* to allow him to understand it in all its tragic fullness. He has, then, the feeling that his brain has become foreign to him and deigns to communicate to him only

> vague, most often incongruous memories. . . . Most of the time it seems content to make mechanical connections between pat notions, to associate words quite aimlessly.[10]

Aimlessly, at the mercy of cruel irony, he approaches the last page of his existence, a blank, in which his intelligence, apparently vast, balks before the impossible inscription of death until biological death arrives. Giving him back his voice, his son introduces this reconstituted autobiography by an injunction which, for me, is one of the most startling messages that a father can transmit to his child:

> You're bored? All you need is to have an inner life! Then you'll never be bored again.[11]

Remarkable, this way of considering boredom, the terrible ennui that dogged Simkha Apatchevsky all his life like some foreign body, a metastasis of the world around him. Isn't it the faculty of keeping faith in the inner life that allows this thoroughly embittered man, this child wounded and betrayed by a mother who dies too early, to wage a fierce struggle against what was imposed upon him like the product of a fatality? But isn't it also because he placed this terrible vexation outside of "his inner life" that he had to wage a struggle he's lost in advance? Isn't it because this outer world was separate,

---

[10] Ibid., 124.

[11] Ibid., 6.

detached from any interiority, that it seemed impossible to invest it libidinally? So the subject, like desperate characters in a Jim Jarmusch film,[12] evolves in a gray world, a black-and-white universe. The only events that gain a certain prominence are those related to the catastrophic perception the melancholic has of his history and his existence. This allows him to play the prophet of doom and to recognize himself in the effects of "melancholization" that the dissolution of social bonds unleashes.

The considerations Pierre Pachet's work raise allow us to recall, as Michaël Löwy and Robert Sayre note, that "Romanticism has from its inception been lit by two lights: the star of revolt and the black sun of melancholy (so dear to Nerval)."[13]

Romanticism, which comes out of a pathos-laden nostalgia for a vanished past, had in fact to continually question a theory of the constitutional state that used categories espoused by Montesquieu and the encyclopedists as a cover for misery, masking the immense disconnection at work in society:

> It is here that Romanticism revealed all its critical power and its lucidity, in the face of the blindness of the ideologies of progress. The Romantic critics hit upon—albeit intuitively or partially—what was unthought in bourgeois thought, they *saw* what lay outside the field of visibility of the world's liberal, individualistic vision: reification, quantification, the loss of qualitative human and cultural values, the solitude of individuals, uprooting, alienation by commodification, the brakeless dynamic of machinism and technology, temporality reduced to the momentary, the degradation of nature.[14]

But just as a diagnosis of melancholia does not mean praise of apathy or death, this vision of society does not represent a condem-

---

[12] Jim Jarmusch, *Stranger Than Paradise* (1984).

[13] Michaël Löwy and Robert Sayre, *Révolte et mélancolie. Le Romantisme à contre-courant de la modernité* (Paris: Payot, 1992), 30.

[14] Ibid., 297–298.

nation of modernity or a prelude to the return of barbarism. The Romantics who, like Walter Benjamin, had an "intuition of the abyss opening up" were alone in perceiving the dangers inherent in the logic of certain modernities. We can only concur with Christa Wolf's statement:

> Numb with disenchantment and petrified, we find ourselves face to face with the objectified dreams of that instrumental thought that continues to swear allegiance to reason but which has long distanced itself from the emancipatory postulate of those Enlightenment thinkers who envisaged a coming-of-age for humanity. With its entry into the industrial era, this thought has changed into sheer utilitarian frenzy.[15]

Let us stress that those who have preached social tension, revolutionary struggle in a Romantic mode (Victor Serge or Durutti, say, but also the Guevarists, or Ben Barka and Lumumba) have by the same impulse deciphered what in the social realm represented a killing off of the subject in the name of the constitutional state and consensus.

Likewise, certain analysts, exalting an ideal of unhappiness and destruction based on theorizations about the subjectivizing function of first mourning for the *infans*, "confusing the case of Dora with the character of Antigone in the name of pure desire,"[16] have spurred on—much to their surprise, yet most often in utter miscalculation of the effects of their discourse—the return of positivism to psychoanalytical theory, a reaction that tends to reject any reference to the death drive or to the theory of the subject in Freudian theory. Nevertheless, the analyst is constantly required to listen to the destructive aspect in the binding of drives that characterizes the subject; and the latter can abandon the past only in making a detour

---

[15] Christa Wolf, *Lesen und Schreiben* (Luchterhanad: Darmstadt and Neuwied, 1984), 320, quoted by M. Löwy and R. Sayre in W. Moser, *Romantisme et crises de la modernité. Poésie et encyclopédie dans le "Brouillon" de Novalis* (Québec: Éditions du Préambule), 299.

[16] Cf. Roland Gori, "Pour se déprendre du discours tragique" (To Move Beyond Tragic Discourse), in "L'inconscient, l'inceste et la dimension du tragique en psychanalyse," *Études freudiennes*, 35 (Paris: May 1994): 173.

through it: thus, in symbolizing, subjectivizing the present. This means, by the same token, emerging from melancholic stasis (or ecstasy). For our part, we can only endorse the concluding statement to Michaël Löwy and Robert Sayre's work:

> Without nostalgia for the past there can be no authentic dream of the future. In this sense, *utopia will be romantic or will not be at all*.[17]

This detour leads me back once more to the question Janus posed from his very first session: Can social ills fail to leave their trace upon the subject? Doesn't this subject tend, when suffering overwhelms him, to invoke the social order, even if it means imputing to it the torments that rack him?

These are all questions I'm inclined to put in perspective with the question of desire, as Lacan does when he elaborates upon his statement, "the pleasure principle is the law of the good,"[18] with the following:

> If happiness is a seamless assent of the subject to his life, as the *Critique*[19] quite classically defines it, it is clear that this is refused to anyone who does not abandon the path of desire.[20]

Thus for Lacan happiness—in its platitude—is the product of a renunciation of desire. This will come as no surprise if we consider that the text "Kant with Sade" dates from the period in which Lacan, by way of Empedocles, was pursuing the myth of a *pure desire*[21] that would represent a failure of the pleasure principle and of happiness.

This pair of opposites opens another set of questions: Does the

---

[17] Löwy and Sayre, *Révolte et mélancolie*, 303.

[18] Jacques Lacan, "Kant avec Sade," in *Écrits* (Paris: Le Seuil, 1966), 766.

[19] Referring, of course, to Kant's *Critique of Pure Reason*.

[20] Lacan, "Kant avec Sade," 785.

[21] He will later abandon this notion. At the end of Seminar XX, *The Four Fundamental Concepts of Psychoanalysis* [original French ed., p. 248], Lacan will write: "The

analyst have something to say about Evil? Can we today question this concept, the way Freud was able to elaborate the question of religion in *The Future of an Illusion* and the problem that the organized masses pose for the analyst in "Group Psychology and the Analysis of the Ego," or as Lacan managed to do by evoking Sade's relation to the Law? In fact, our question is consonant with the one the divine marquis posed for Lacan:

> Sade therefore stopped there, at the point where desire is tied to the Law. Could something in him still be bound up by the Law, to find there the occasion Saint Paul speaks of, of being a boundless sinner who would cast the first stone? But he wasn't further off. It isn't just that in him, as in anyone, the flesh is weak, it's that the mind is too quick not to be deceived. The apology for crime forces him only to the avowal diverted by the Law. The supreme Being is restored in Evil-Doing."[22]

Now quoting Paul Ricoeur, Denis Rosenfield recalls that "evil is an act that each individual initiates." It seems crucial to me that a *point of origin* should be invoked here at the moment that

> . . . evil . . . is engendered by human action both in its individual dimension and in its collective dimension, thereby allowing for a new beginning, for something created.[23]

Indeed, Evil, at once breaking the social contract and the code of laws that over the millennia has allowed the formation of the collective,[24] lends transparency to a new order against a background

---

22 Lacan, "Kant avec Sade," 789–790.

23 Denis Rosenfield, *Du mal. Essai pour introduire en philosophie le concept du mal* (Paris: Aubier, 1990), 169.

24 Here we shall distinguish the notion of the "collective" from that of the masses or the crowd.

of tabula rasa, an order in which desire can apparently no longer be questioned, so far does it seem to exceed the human and the thinkable to the point of changing the known forms of transgression.

> This signifies that there is a specific type of transgression that not only has individual impact, that is not solely the negation of something given, but that occurs both on an individual and collective level as necessarily malign and which, by this fact, offends against the very principle of human rationality. . . . Its goal is not merely the transgression of this or that rule, but of what falls short of any rule, by its common constitutive and founding principle. . . .
> At the level of understanding, malign transgression is thus an action that achieves a real and positive negation of man's being, which does not, in principle, exclude the insane attempt to found a non-humanity, that is, a humanity whose rules—if one can still use this term—would have no goal but to let mankind function as a beast-machine, utterly passive and controllable.[25]

A mass of inexpressible violence, of absolute cruelty and deep melancholy, Françoise, a Jew from the Avignon area, is literally a product of the Nazi horror. Her mother having been deported while pregnant to Germany, then to a ghetto in Eastern Europe, Françoise was born when Soviet troops were advancing upon Berlin. For over fifty years she has been confronted with what Rosenfield cites by reference to Schelling and Hegel, who attained their highest reflection on the question of evil:

> The problem is especially interesting here because "wickedness" has not been attributed to the resurgence of the ancient conception of human nature, nor to the resurrection of what was abolished historically, nor to the presence of animal, sensory, or passional part of human beings: it is situated in freedom, it occurs as the perversion of a rule or of mankind's inherent capacity to impose rules on itself.[26]

---

[25] Rosenfield, *Du mal*, 165–167.

[26] Ibid., 41.

Actually, what so outrages Françoise is the slippage that occurs today in what she perceives as absolute perversion: the cult of the *Same*. This Same, mind you, is not the mob or crowd that, to the sound of an electrifying, rigidifying voice, marches at the heels of some great helmsman, f ührer, or *Conducator*. No, this Same is now the consensual one of coexistence, of a tension reduction no jolt could possibly reanimate. It is the reign of stasis, inertia, false freedom, the kind that thrives in a Mitteleuropa that authorizes all sorts of proliferations. It's the reign of the two-dimensional image, robbed of its shadow and its symbolic dimension, forbidding the utterance of real words, that is, in the *Witz*, the joke, the play of wit.

It is deadly, this utter lack of contradiction for the sake of the smile that corpses sport in funeral homes. Deadly, this refusal to leave visible traces of any ill on a body now conceived as a hunk of meat endowed with eternal youth. Such an erasure denies death for the sake of the clean, of what isn't ugly, of the politically correct; in short, it's *Cotard syndrome* dished up as the highest form of social ideal.

One must also consider that the value accorded to stasis, to immortality, to correction, soothes the feeling of unshakable good conscience typified by anti-Germanic racism[27]: "Only the Germans are responsible for this eruption of barbarism, only circumstances imposed upon us and supported by a fringe of French fascists, readers of the *Gringoire* and *Je suis partout,* can implicate us in this genocide, in which, in any case, we did not participate"—so runs the refrain that especially drives Françoise crazy. It took the French Republic's official acknowledgment through the voice of its President of the wrong that Françoise and her kind had suffered at the hands of some citizens of this country she passionately loves, for something to crack and give way in her—for her finally to say what about her relation to others and in the causes of the social bond could strike her at the core of her being, assail her at the depths of

---

[27] Jean Baudrillard, *La Transparence du mal. Essai sur les phénomènes extrêmes* (Paris: Galilée, 1990), 75.

what we'll call the binding of drives, at a time when the good conscience of her compatriots seemed every day to signify that her outcry could only fall on deaf ears. This denial had struck with full force at what Françoise called her "innermost being," making any thought of otherness impossible.

Far more, the consensus preached by the well-meaning had roused a central concern of hers: the eruption that claims to abolish extremes and tensions seemed likely to her to endanger the limits of her body, raising the terrifying risk of triumphant asexuality. The eruption of the sexless seemed to her to be the offshoot of what, in the social, proves to be the product of a possible reciprocity that claims that—all things being equal, after all—the crime did not take place, and even if it had taken place, it would merely have been the crime that pitted omnipotent supermen against survivors whom their former persecutors persistently present as ghosts if not vampires, after having considered them vermin.

So, denial of a historical sequence or an ever-possible regression of the constitutional state in the name of right, raises the question of the reappearance on the social scene of the unorganized mob rigidified by the baneful return of God[28] or the ultimate guarantee of "consensuality."

Literature and clinical practice teach us: If melancholics in their solitude are subjectively prey to an inability to mourn and the denial of a death which seems to have always existed, they are also—like certain authors whose tales capture the infinite, desperate disquiet society rouses in them[29]—closest to the new "discontent in civilization," the one that laughably greets massacre with humanitarianism and mass crime with denial.

Now, if strictly speaking there is no such thing as a melancholic

---

[28] Jacques Lacan, *Télévision* (Paris: Le Seuil, 1974), 54.

[29] Cf. Thomas Bernhard in relation to post-war Austrian society, Franz Kafka to the early advent of mechanized, massified death, Paul Celan or Primo Levi racked by the insurmountability of Evil they experienced with their own flesh.

society, but only urban sites dominated by *le Mal*,[30] the fact still remains that institutions, countries, if not whole continents are witnessing an assault upon the social bond such that in their very lap, as it were, we can sight some of the cardinal symptoms of melancholy, symptoms beside which Franco's *Viva la muerte* is but a murmur.

There remains the question those authors pose to us whose works seem marked by melancholy. I have suggested that each of these bodies of work is in itself an attempt to create a proper object—an object of one's own—enabling the work of mourning, a mourning that is accomplished thanks to the written text which, in being published, is thus offered to th᾽ Other. Yet this activity, pervaded by a sublime melancholy, remains unresolved, as though each time the object could not be established. Writing, rather than producing a solace, actually fosters the enigma of an unfathomable cruelty, similar to the one melancholics inflict upon themselves, having been forever confronted with a loss whose profile they can't trace. Isn't this, after all, what prompts the melancholic poet to say:

> *I am the wound and the knife!* . . .
> *Victim and hangman alike.*[31]

or might prompt some other writer to make a motto of this terrible sentence of Maurice Blanchot:

> Apathy is the spirit of negation applied to one who has chosen sovereignty.[32]

---

30 Cf. Jean Baudrillard, *La Transparence du mal* and Bernard Edelman, *L'Homme des foules* (Paris: Petite Bibliothèque Payot, 1981).

31 Charles Baudelaire, "L'Héautontimorouménos," *Les Fleurs du mal* (Flowers of Evil) in *Œuvres complètes* (Paris: Gallimard, "Bibl. de la Pléiade," 1968), 74.

32 Maurice Blanchot, quoted by Georges Bataille in *Œuvres complètes*, vol. VIII, *L'Histoire de l'érotisme* (Paris: Gallimard, 1976), 153.

Bibliography

Abraham, H. C. and E. L. Freud, eds. *A Psycho-Analytic Dialogue: The Letters of Sigmund Freud and Karl Abraham, 1907–1926.* New York: Basic Books, 1965.

Bataille, Georges. *Œuvres complètes,* vol. VIII. Paris: Gallimard, 1976.

Baudrillard, Jean. *La Transparence du mal: Essai sur les phénomènes extrêmes.* Paris: Galilée, 1990.

Baudry, François. *L'Intime.* Paris: Éditions de l'Éclat, 1988.

Bernhard, Thomas. *Je te salue Virgile.* Paris: Gallimard, 1988.

Clavreul, Jean. "Les pervers de la loi du désir." *L'Inconscient, Revue de Psychanalyse,* no. 2, April/June 1967; reprinted in *Le Désir et la Loi.* Paris: Denoël, 1987.

Cocteau, Jean. *Opium, The Diary of a Cure.* Translated by Margaret Crosland and Sinclair Road. New York: Grove Press, 1958.

Colli, Giorgio. *La Sagesse grecque,* vol. III ("Héraclite"). Paris: Éditions de l'Éclat, 1992.

Dostoyevsky, Fyodor. *Notes from Underground / The Double.* Translated by Jessie Coulson. New York: Penguin Books, 1972.

Edelman, Bernard. *L'Homme des foules.* Paris: Petite Bibliothèque Payot, 1981.

Feijo, Benito. *Le Je-ne-sais-quoi.* Translated by Catherine Paoletti. Paris: Éditions de l'Éclat, 1989.

Fournier, Jacques. *Régistre d'inquisition de [Bishop of Pamiers] 1318–1325.* Translated and annotated by Jean Duvernoy. Paris: École des hautes études en sciences sociales, 1979.

Freud, Sigmund. "Mourning and Melancholia." Translated by Joan Riviere. *General Psychological Theory.* New York: Collier Books (1963): 164–179.

————. *Beyond the Pleasure Principle.* Translated by James Strachey. New York: W. W. Norton & Co., 1961.

————. "Reflections Upon War and Death." Translated by E. Colburn Mayne, reprinted in *Character and Culture*. New York: Collier Books (1963): 107–133.

————. *The Problem of Anxiety* [original: *Hemmung, Symptom und Angst*]. Translated by Henry Alden Bunker. New York: W. W. Norton & Co., 1936. Also: *Inhibitions, Symptoms, and Anxiety. Standard Edition*, vol. 20, 87–172. London: Hogarth Press, 1959.

————. "The Economic Problem of Masochism." Translated by Joan Riviere. *General Psychological Theory.* New York: Collier Books (1963): 190–201.

————. *Totem and Taboo: Some Points of Agreement Between the Mental Lives of Savages and Neurotics.* Translated by James Strachey. New York: W. W. Norton & Co., 1950.

Geberovich, Fernando. *Une douleur irrésistible.* Paris: Inter-Éditions, 1984.

El-Hakim, Tawfik. *Journal d'un substitut de campagne.* Paris: Plon, 1974.

Hassoun, Jacques. *Fragments de langue maternelle.* Paris: Payot, 1979. Second edition, Paris: Point Hors Ligne, 1993.

————. *Les Passions intraitables.* Paris: Aubier, 1993.

Ingold, F.-R. "La dépendance," in "Drogue et société," *Esprit,* no. 11–12 (Nov.–Dec. 1980).

Jankélévitch, Vladimir. *Le Je-ne-sais-quoi et le Presque rien.* Paris: Le Seuil, 1980.

Kafka, Franz. "The Hunter Gracchus," *Selected Short Stories.* Translated by Willa and Edwin Muir. New York: The Modern Library, 1993.

Lacan, Jacques. *Le Séminaire, Livre XX, Encore, 1962–63.* Edited by Jacques-Alain Miller. Paris: Le Seuil, 1975.

————. *Le Séminaire, Livre VII, L'éthique de la psychanalyse, 1950–60.* Edited by Jacques-Alain Miller. Paris: Le Seuil, 1986. [*The Seminar, Book VII, The Ethics of Psychoanalysis, 1959–60.* Translated by Dennis Porter. London: Routledge, 1992.]

————. *Le Séminaire, Livre X, L'angoisse, 1962–63,* unpublished.

————. *Le Séminaire, Livre VIII, Le transfert, 1960–61.* Edited by Jacques-Alain Miller. Paris: Le Seuil, 1991.

————. "Kant avec Sade," *Écrits.* Paris: Le Seuil, 1966.

————. "The Signification of the Phallus," *Écrits: A Selection.* Translated by Alan Sheridan. New York: W. W. Norton & Co., 1977.

————. "La science et la vérité," *Écrits.* Paris: Le Seuil, 1966.

————. "Les Complexes familiaux dans la formation de l'individu. Essai d'analyse d'une fonction en psychologie," *Encyclopédie française* (Paris, 1938) [Reprinted, Paris: Éditions Navarin, 1984].

————. *Le Séminaire, Livre XI, Les quatre concepts fondamentaux de la psychanalyse, 1964.* Edited by Jacques-Alain Miller. Paris: Le Seuil, 1973. [*The Four Fundamental Concepts of Psychoanalysis.* Translated by Alan Sheridan. New York: W. W. Norton & Co., 1978.]

Levi, Primo. *Survival in Auschwitz.* Translated by Stuart Woolf. New York: Collier Books, 1961.

Louÿs, Pierre. *La Femme et le Pantin.* Paris: Albin Michel, 1977.

Löwy, Michaël and Robert Sayre. *Révolte et mélancolie: Le Romantisme à contre-courant de la modernité.* Paris: Payot, 1992.

Melville, Herman. "Bartleby," *Billy Budd and Other Stories.* New York: Penguin Books, 1986.

Mongin, Olivier. "L'esprit de la loi dans les sociétés modernes, culpabilité ou responsabilité," in *Esprit*, no. 11–12 (Nov.–Dec. 1980), 148.

Munier, Roger. *Mélancolie.* Paris: Le Nyctalope, 1987.

Ocampo, Victoria. *L'Envers de la toxicomanie.* Paris: Denoël, 1989.

Pachet, Pierre. *Autobiographie de mon père.* Paris: Autrement-Littératures, 1994.

Paxton, Robert O. *Vichy France: Old Guard and New Order, 1940–1944.* New York: Knopf, 1972.

Perrier, François. *La Chaussée d'Antin,* 2 volumes, 10/18 (1978), 67, quoted by François Baudry, *L'Intime.* Paris: Éditions de l'Éclat, 1988.

Préaud, Maxime. *Mélancolies.* Paris: Éditions Herscher, 1982.

Proust, Marcel, *Swann's Way,* vol. 1 of *Remembrance of Things Past.* Translated by C. K. Scott Moncrieff and Terence Kilmartin. New York: Vintage Books, 1982.

Rosenfield, Denis. *Du mal: Essai pour introduire en philosophie le concept du mal.* Paris: Aubier, 1989.

Tsvetaeva, Marina. *Neuf lettres avec une dixième retenue et une onzième reçue.* Paris: Clémence Hiver, 1985.

Walser, Robert, *Institute Benjamenta.* Translated by Christopher Middleton. London: Serpent's Tail Press, 1995.

Wolf, Christa. *Lesen und Schreiben.* Darmstadt and Neuwied, Luchterhand. Quoted in Moser, Walter, *Romantisme et crises de la modernité: Poésie et encyclopédie dans le "Brouillon" de Novalis.* Longueuil, Québec: Le Préambule, 1989.